THE COOK'S ENCYCLOPEDIA OF
COOKIES

THE COOK'S ENCYCLOPEDIA OF

COOKIES

HILAIRE WALDEN

BARNES
&NOBLE
BOOKS
NEW YORK

This edition published by Barnes & Noble, Inc.,
by arrangement with Anness Publishing Limited

2002 Barnes & Noble Books

M 10 9 8 7 6 5 4 3 2

ISBN 0 7607 3095 4

Publisher: Joanna Lorenz
Project Editor: Joanne Rippin
Designer: Siân Keogh, Axis Design
Illustrator: Christos Chrysanthou, Axis design

Previously published as *The Great Big Cookie Book*

Printed and bound in China

NOTES
Standard spoon and cup measures are level.
Large eggs are used unless otherwise stated.

The recipes in this book were supplied by: Liz Trigg, Patricia Lousada, Carla Capalbo, Laura Washburn, Frances Cleary, Norma MacMillan, Christine France,
Pamela Westland, Hilaire Walden, Elizabeth Wolf-Cohen, Janice Murfitt, Carole Handslip, Steven Wheeler, Katherine Richmond, Joanna Farrow, Judy Williams,
Sue Maggs, Carole Clements, Jacqueline Clark, Sarah Maxwell, Sallie Morris, Lesley Mackley, Roz Denny, Sarah Gates, Norma Miller, Maxine Clark, Shirley Gill,
Judy Jackson, Gilly Love, Janet Brinkworth, Ruby Le Bois, Elisabeth Lambert Ortiz, Sohelia Kimberley.

Photography by: Karl Adamson, Edward Allright, Steve Baxter, James Duncan, John Freeman, Michelle Garrett, Nelson Hargreaves, Amanda Heywood,
David Jordan, Patrick McLeavey, Michael Michaels, Polly Wreford.

Contents

6
Introduction

8
Cookie Tips and Techniques

28
Traditional Cookies

72
Festive and Fancy Cookies

118
Savory Treats

150
Brownies and Bars

184
Muffins and Scones

216
Cookies for Kids

236
Cookie Treats and Gifts

254
Index

Introduction

The word cookie has become quite common throughout the world; here we present cookies in their many guises.

The word "cookie" is of Dutch origin, from the word *koekje* meaning little cake. The origins of the British term for cookie, biscuit, are to be found in the word itself: it comes from the French *bis cuit,* meaning twice cooked, and goes back to the days when bakers put slices of newly baked bread back into the oven, so that they dried out completely, becoming something like a rusk. This was really a method of preservation, for it enabled the cookies to be kept for a long time; so long, in fact, that they could be taken as a basic food item, known as "ships biscuits," on long sea voyages.

For many years cooks and housewives continued the practice of drying their biscuits a second time, and it was not until the beginning of the last century that the habit died out. Then both the quality and variety of biscuits that could be made improved dramatically.

Now there are many names and forms for cookies, but usually they are individual, small, crisp baked cakes. We call them cookies when they are sweet, crackers when savory, while in Britain both cookies and crackers are called biscuits. To add to the confusion, we call biscuits what the British generally call scones, while we usually agree on what we call muffins. Happily, the distinctions are blurring, and in this *Great Big Cookie Book* you will find the truth in the baking and tasting of the many cookies, biscuits, crackers, muffins and scones described here.

We have collected cookies from all over the world, family favorites for generations, classic recipes for holidays and celebrations, and national specialties that have crossed many borders, such as Amaretti from Italy, Basbousa from the Middle East and Oatcakes from Scotland. Here you will find a homemade cookie for every occasion. And homemade cookies put the store-bought to shame; a batch of cookies ready to come out of the oven will fill your kitchen with a wonderful aroma, followed by the unbeatable taste of your own fresh-baked creation.

Finally, cookies are easy and fun to make. You can make them alone to cheer up a rainy day, or share the enjoyment with your family and friends, especially fun at holiday times. So, turn the pages of this book with anticipation of the many treats to come.

▶ *Cookies are not only ideal for everyday eating or special treats at home; they can also be gift wrapped and given away as a special gift.*

Cookie Tips & Techniques

Cookies can be made using a wide variety of methods to suit all ranges of ability and to match the time and ingredients available. Most cookies are easy to make and special skills are rarely required. But, as with most things, once you know exactly the right way to do something, it becomes that much quicker, easier and enjoyable, and the results are far more likely to be successful. The following pages in the Cookie Tips & Techniques section provide all the information you will need to make successful cookies every time, with the minimum amount of effort.

You will find advice on choosing the most appropriate ingredients for the particular cookie you are making, and handy tips on how to carry out simple but vital tasks like measuring accurately. There are detailed instructions for all the methods used for making and shaping cookies, including piping the raw mixture, as well as the various methods of melting chocolate. Ideas for making cookies look really attractive are also included, and the way to make piping bags from greaseproof paper is described.

There are also recommendations on storing the cookies so they will remain fresh for as long as possible, plus ideas on how to wrap and present your cookies so they become special gifts with a strong personal feel.

The Pantry

The ingredients for cookie making can be found in most people's pantries and refrigerators.

Chocolate Buy good quality chocolate with at least 50% cocoa solids for baking. Semisweet chocolate gives a distinctive strong, rich flavor while milk chocolate has a sweeter taste. White chocolate often does not contain any cocoa solids and lacks the flavor of true chocolate. It is the most difficult chocolate to melt and has poor setting qualities.

Eggs Eggs should be at room temperature so, if you keep them in the refrigerator, remove the number you want at least 30 minutes before making a recipe.

Dried fruits Today, most dried fruits are dried by artificial heat rather than by the sun, and are treated with sulphur dioxide to help their preservation. Oils are sometimes sprayed onto the fruit to give it a shiny appearance and to prevent it from sticking. Try to buy fruit that has been coated with vegetable oils, not mineral oils.

Butter and margarine Butter gives the best flavor to cookies and should be used whenever possible, especially when there is a high fat content, as in shortbread. However, it can be used interchangeably with hard margarine. Butter or margarine to be used for creaming with sugar needs to be at room temperature and softened. For rubbing in, it should be at a cool room temperature, not refrigerator hard, and chopped quite finely.

Soft margarine is really only suitable for making cookies by the all-in-one method and when the fat has to be melted.

Flours Flour provides the structure that makes the cookies. Always sift flour. Not only will this remove any lumps, which are rare nowadays, but it lightens the flour by incorporating air and makes it easier to mix in.

Self-rising flour has rising agents added and is the type of flour most usually used in straightforward cookies that need to rise.

All-purpose flour is used when rising is considered a fault, as when making shortbread. Rich or heavy mixtures that should be raised also often call for all-purpose flour plus additional rising agents in the specific proportions required for the particular recipe.

Wholewheat flour adds more flavor than white flour and is the healthier option but does produce denser cookies. When lightness is important extra rising agents should be added. Some recipes work well with a mixture of white and whole wheat flour.

Candied fruits Wash candied fruits before using them to remove the syrupy coating, then dry thoroughly.

Spices Ground cinnamon, ginger, apple pie or pumpkin pie spice, nutmeg and cloves may be used in cookies. All spices should be as fresh as possible. Buy in small quantities, and keep in a cool, dark, dry place.

Honey Honey adds its own distinctive flavor to cookies. It contains 17% water so you will need to use slightly more honey than sugar, and reduce the amounts of the other liquids used. Use honey within a few months of opening, and keep in a cool, dark, dry place.

Sugars Granulated sugar is the best sweetener to use for the creaming method because the crystals dissolve easily and quickly when creamed with the fat. Granulated sugar can also be used for rubbed-in mixtures and when the sugar is heated with the fat or liquid until it dissolves. Confectioners' sugar appears in the ingredients for some cookie recipes where it is important that the sugar dissolves very readily. Demerara sugar can be used when the sugar is dissolved over heat before being added to the dry ingredients. Soft light and dark brown sugars are used when a richer flavor and color are called for. Raw sugar is unrefined sugar which is uncolored and pure.

Nuts Nuts become rancid if stored for too long, in the light or at too high a temperature, so only buy in amounts that you will use within 1-2 months and keep them in an airtight container in a cool, dark cupboard. Alternatively, freeze them for up to 1 year.

Equipment

A delightful aspect of cookie making is that it requires a minimum of special equipment.

You can make a wide range of cookies with just a mixing bowl, measures or weights, a wooden spoon, a baking sheet and a wire rack. Only a few items are needed to extend the range much further. Many supermarkets now sell all you will need for cookie making.

Baking sheets Use good-quality sturdy sheets; thin, cheap sheets will buckle with time. Cheap sheets also heat more quickly so cookies are liable to cook quickly, brown and stick to them more readily. Nonstick sheets, of course, save greasing and lining when called for, greatly reduce sticking and cut down on washing up.

Cannelle knife This tool is great for carving stripes in the skin of citrus fruit. Pare off thin strips before slicing the fruit to make an attractive edge.

Cutters Cutters are available in many different shapes and sizes, ranging from simple plain cookie circles to small cutters for *petits fours* and savory cocktail nibbles, to animal shapes, hearts and flowers. For best results, the important criterion that applies to all cutters is that they should be sharp to give a good, clear, outline. This really means that they should be made from metal; plastic cutters tend to compress the cut edges.

To use a cutter, press down firmly on the cutter so that it cuts straight down right through the dough. Then lift up the cutter, without twisting it.

If you want to cut out a shape for which you do not have a cutter, the thing to do is to make a template, or pattern. This is very easy.

Trace or draw the design onto waxed paper or cardboard and cut it out using scissors. Lay the template on the rolled-out cookie dough. Use the point of a large, sharp knife to carefully cut around the template, taking care not to drag it. With a thin metal spatula, transfer the shape to the prepared baking sheet, without distorting the shape.

Food processor Although food processors save time, their drawback is their very speed; they work so fast that you must be careful not to overmix a mixture. Food processors combine rather than beat ingredients together, so they are not so useful for recipes where lightness is important. Also, many models cannot beat egg whites, and even in those designed for beating, the whites will not become really stiff.

Knives A table knife can be used for the initial stages of cutting in the fat before it is rubbed in. Large, sharp knives are needed for cutting cleanly and efficiently through rolled-out dough or refrigerated dough. Metal spatulas are invaluable for spreading and smoothing mixtures in cake pans, transferring cut-out cookies to baking sheets before baking and then transferring the baked cookies to a wire rack to cool. They can also be used for spreading icing on cookies.

Measures A set of accurate measuring spoons is vital for measuring 1 tablespoon, 1 teaspoon and fractions of teaspoons. All the amounts given in recipes are for level spoonfuls unless otherwise stated. For liquids, use a heatproof measuring cup, preferably see-through in 1-cup, 2-cup and 4-cup sizes.

Pastry brushes A large pastry brush is very useful for brushing surplus flour from work surfaces and cookie doughs that are being rolled out, and for greasing cake pans. A pastry brush is also needed for brushing on glazes. Buy good-quality brushes with firmly fixed bristles.

Piping bags and nozzles A medium icing bag with a selection of nozzles is very useful to have for piping uncooked cookie dough and for decorating cookies after baking. Use small disposable icing bags for chocolate or icing, where a fine line is required.

Rolling pin Rolling pins made of wood are the most common, but you can now buy marble or even plastic ones which are considered to be more hygienic.

Scales A good set of scales is essential for successful cookie making. Whether you use spring balance, modern electronic or old-fashioned balanced scales with a set of weights, test them frequently for accuracy by putting something on them which has the weight printed on it.

Sieves If possible have a set of strong sieves in 2 or 3 different sizes.

Skewers and toothpicks Either of these can be used for testing whether cookie mixtures are cooked.

Spatulas A flexible rubber spatula is indispensable for scraping every last morsel from the mixing bowl onto the baking sheet.

Swivel-blade peelers Both long-handled and broad-handled peelers are the best tools for peeling fruit.

Tea strainer A tea strainer will come in handy for sifting icing sugar over cookies as a last-minute decoration.

Whisk Use either a wire balloon whisk or a rotary whisk for beating eggs together. It is a good idea to have two sizes of balloon whisks, to suit the amount of mixture.

Zester Ideal for citrus fruit, a zester has the same function as a cannelle knife but produces a row of thin stripes.

Measuring ingredients

Cooks with years of experience may not need to measure ingredients, but if you are a beginner or are trying a new recipe for the first time, it is best to follow instructions carefully. Also, measuring ingredients precisely will ensure consistent results.

1 For liquids measured in cups or pints: use a glass or clear plastic measuring cup. Put it on a flat surface and pour in the liquid. Bend down and check that the liquid is level with the marking on the cup, as specified in the recipe.

2 For liquids measured in spoons: pour the liquid into the measuring spoon, to the brim, and then pour it into the mixing bowl. Do not hold the spoon over the bowl when measuring because some liquid may overflow.

3 For measuring dry ingredients in a spoon: fill the spoon, scooping up the ingredient. Level the surface to the rim of the spoon, using the straight edge of a knife.

4 For measuring dry ingredients by weight: scoop or pour onto the scales, watching the dial or reading carefully. Balance scales give more accurate readings than spring scales.

5 For measuring syrups: grease the inside of a measuring cup before pouring in the required weight of syrup.

6 For measuring butter: cut with a sharp knife and weigh, or cut off the specified amount following the markings on the wrapping paper.

Making cookies by the rubbing in method

Plain cookies are usually made by rubbing the fat into the flour. For this, the fat, whether butter, margarine or lard, should be neither rock hard from the refrigerator, nor too warm. It is first chopped into small pieces, then added to the dry ingredients in a bowl. The mixture is lifted high and the lumps of fat rubbed between the fingertips as the mixture is allowed to fall back into the bowl.

1 Sift the flour into a bowl, adding the raising agents, salt and any sugar or spices and mix them evenly.

2 Stir in any other dry ingredients; combine the oats or other cereal, or coconut. Add the butter or margarine, cut into pieces.

3 Sprinkle the liquid ingredients (water, cream, milk, buttermilk or beaten egg) over the mixture.

4 Stir with a fork until the dry ingredients are thoroughly moistened and will come together in a ball of fairly soft dough in the center of the bowl.

5 Press the dough into a ball. If it is too dry to form a dough, add some extra water.

6 Turn the dough onto a lightly floured surface. Knead very lightly, folding and pressing, to mix evenly – about 30 seconds. Wrap the ball of dough in plastic wrap or waxed paper and chill it for at least 30 minutes.

Making cookies by the creaming method

To make cookies by the creaming method, the fat and sugar are "creamed" – or beaten – together before the eggs and dry ingredients are added. The fat (usually butter or margarine) should be soft enough to be beaten so, if necessary, remove it from the refrigerator and leave for at least 30 minutes. For best results, the eggs should be at room temperature.

1 Sift the flour with the salt, raising agent(s) and any other dry ingredients, such as spices or cocoa powder, into a bowl. Set aside.

2 Put the fat in a large, deep bowl and beat with an electric mixer at medium speed, or a wooden spoon, until the texture is soft and pliable.

3 Add the sugar to the creamed fat gradually. With the mixer at medium-high speed, or using the wooden spoon, beat it into the fat until the mixture is pale and very fluffy. The sugar should be completely incorporated.

5 Add the dry ingredients to the mixture. Beat at low speed just until smoothly combined, or fold in with a large metal spoon.

6 If the recipe calls for any liquid, add it in small portions alternately with portions of the dry ingredients.

7 If the recipe specifies, beat egg whites separately until frothy, add sugar and continue whisking until stiff peaks form. Fold into the mixture.

Making cookies by the all-in-one method

Some cookies are made by an easy all-in-one method where all the ingredients are combined in a bowl and beaten thoroughly. The mixture can also be made in a food processor, but take care not to over-process. A refinement on the all-in-one method is to separate the eggs and make the mixture with the yolks. The whites are whisked separately and then folded in. Soft margarine has to be used.

4 Add the eggs or egg yolks, one at a time, beating well after each addition. Scrape the bowl often so all the ingredients are evenly combined. If the mixture curdles, add 1 tbsp of the measured flour.

1 Sift the flour and any other dry ingredients such as salt, raising agents and spices, into a bowl.

2 Add the liquid ingredients, such as eggs, melted or soft fat, milk or fruit juices, and beat until smooth, with an electric mixer for speed. Pour into the prepared pans and bake as specified in the recipe.

8 Pour the mixture into a prepared cake pan and bake as specified.

Rolling and cutting cookies

A cookie dough that is to be rolled and cut must have the right consistency; if it is too dry it will crumble, crack and be difficult to roll neatly, whereas if it is too wet it will stick when rolled out and will spread during baking.

1 After mixing, knead the cookie dough lightly so it holds together, then wrap it in plastic wrap or waxed paper and chill it for at least 1 hour. To speed the chilling, put the dough in the freezer for 30 minutes. Tap over the dough with a rolling pin to flatten it, then gently roll out the dough with short, light strokes in one direction to the required thickness.

2 Doughs that are stiff enough to roll may be cut with a knife into squares, rectangles, triangles or fingers, or they can be stamped into rounds or fancy shapes using cutters. To prevent sticking, sprinkle the work surface generously with flour or sugar, according to the recipe, before rolling out the dough, and use a floured or sugared rolling pin.

3 Position the floured cutter near the outside edge of the dough and cut out the shape. Continue cutting out shapes, each time placing the cutter close to the cut-out holes, to minimize trimmings. Carefully transfer to the prepared baking sheet. Glaze with beaten egg and sprinkle with nuts, seeds or cheese, if used.

Shaping drop cookies

1 Drop cookies are made from a number of different mixtures, but they invite the use of coarse-textured oats, nuts and dried fruits that cannot be piped through a nozzle. Drop cookies are easy to shape; spoonfuls of mixture are simply dropped onto the prepared baking sheet.

2 Leave plenty of space between the cookies because they spread during cooking. If a mixture is stiff it will have to be spread with the back of a teaspoon or fork, but this is not usually necessary. Drop teaspoons of the mixture onto the prepared baking sheet, spacing them well apart.

Shaping tuiles & cigarettes

Delicate drop cookies, such as Tuiles d'amandes and Brandy Snaps, can be a challenge to the cook. The mixture is particularly thin and a tablespoon or less of flour or liquid can make the difference between success and failure.

1 Roll spoonfuls of the dough into balls and place 1–2 inches apart on the prepared baking sheets.

2 Bake until golden brown, 8–10 minutes. With a metal spatula transfer to a rolling pin to shape, then leave to cool.

Molding cookies

Doughs that are too rich to roll out can be shaped by hand. Some recipes call for moistening your hands with water before handling the dough, others recommend lightly flouring your hands, or using cocoa powder or sugar.

1 Take walnut-size pieces of dough and roll into smooth balls between the palms of your hands. Set them spaced well apart on the prepared baking sheet.

2 Flatten the balls with the back of the tines of a wetted fork to give a lined effect. Alternatively, the base of a greased glass dipped in superfine or confectioners' sugar can be used.

Making refrigerator cookies

These are so called because the dough must be thoroughly chilled before it can be cut into slices for baking, and also because the dough can be conveniently kept in the refrigerator for up to a week before it is baked. The dough can also be frozen and used straight from the freezer, using a good sharp knife.

Refrigerator cookies are simple to make because the chilled logs are firm and easy to slice. They are also time-saving because you can make the roll ahead and slice off just as many cookies as you need at any time. Use a thin, sharp knife and wet the knife occasionally to help to give a smooth, clean cut.

The thickness of the slices determines the character of baked cookies: very thin slices will bake into thin, crisp cookies; thick slices result in thicker, more chewy cookies. Place 1 inch apart on the baking sheets, which are usually ungreased.

1 Beat together the butter and sugar until light and fluffy. Add the flour in three batches, folding in well between each addition. Add any other ingredients and stir in gently.

2 Divide the dough in half and shape each half into a log about 2 inches in diameter. Wrap in waxed paper and chill overnight. Preheat the oven to 375°F. Lightly grease two baking sheets.

3 Cut the dough logs across into slices about 1/8 inch thick. Place on the prepared baking sheets. Bake for about 10 minutes, until just golden around the edges. Transfer to a wire rack to cool.

Piping cookies

The mixture for piped cookies needs to be soft enough to pipe, but it should not be too loose or it will spread and lose its shape during baking. You will need a piping bag of an appropriate size and a large nozzle, either plain or star-shaped, depending on the effect you want to produce (obviously, a star nozzle will give a more decorative appearance). Drop the piping nozzle into the piping bag and twist, tucking the bag into the nozzle. This will prevent any filling from leaking out at the bottom.

1 Fold the top of the bag over your hand to form a collar, or stand the bag in a tall glass. Add the mixture, scraping the spoon or spatula against your hand or the side of the glass. When the bag is one-half to two-thirds full, twist the top until there is no air left.

2 Hold the twisted end of the bag firmly in one hand. Use the other hand to lightly guide the nozzle. Exert a very firm, steady pressure and start to pipe. The trick is to keep the pressure steady until the design is finished. A sudden squeeze will produce a large blob rather than an even flow.

3 As soon as the shape is complete, stop applying pressure, push down slightly and quickly lift up the nozzle.

4 The bag is kept upright for piping swirls, stars or rosettes, but to make straight lines it is held at an angle.

Making a waxed paper icing bag

Waxed paper icing bags are particularly good for piping small quantities
of icing or when two or more colors of icing are being used at once.
They are also easy to use for any type of icing. The bag can be used without
a piping nozzle for making simple, plain lines, or it can be fitted with any size of nozzle.
It is a good idea to make several of these bags at a time.

1 Cut a piece of good quality waxed paper to a 10-inch square. Fold in half to form a triangle.

2 Fold the short side of the triangle over to the right-angled corner to form a cone.

3 Holding the cone together with one hand, wrap the long point of the triangle around the paper cone.

Tip To use the bag for piping, do not overfill it; instead, open it carefully and refill it when necessary, taking care not to split it or let it unfold. The filled bag can be kept in a plastic bag for a few hours.

4 Tuck the point of paper inside the cone to secure it. For extra security, clear tape can be used to hold the paper together. Add the icing, then cut a small, straight piece off the end of the bag.

5 For using with a nozzle, cut off the pointed end of the bag and position the nozzle so that it fits snugly into the point before adding the icing.

Decorating cookies with icing

It is very easy to turn plain cookies into special-looking treats, whether for a children's birthday party or to give as a present to an adult. All that is needed is some icing – you don't even have to do any piping. However, it is a very simple matter to add a little piped icing. There's no need to be adept at icing – the surfaces you will be covering are small so it won't matter if the lines are squiggly.

Icing glaze This is like glacé icing but is thinned with egg white so that it sets, making a thin, tangy cookie glaze.

1 tbsp lightly beaten egg white
1 tbsp lemon juice
³/₄–1 cup confectioners' sugar
Mix the egg white and lemon juice in a bowl. Beat in the confectioners' sugar gradually, until the mixture is smooth with the consistency of thin cream. The icing should coat the back of a spoon.

A very easy way to decorate the tops of cookies is to spread the icing over the top, using a palette knife.

Another very straightforward way to ice the tops of cookies is to just dip them in the icing.

Stenciling

A simple yet effective way to decorate cookies is to pipe lines of a contrasting color backwards and forwards across the top of the baked cookies. With just a few simple, short lines you can add the finishing touches to some spectacular cookies.

A portion of the raw cookie mixture can be colored then piped over the shaped, but still unbaked cookies, so the design is baked in the cookies.

Stenciling is a fun way to liven up cookies. There are no hard and fast rules – experiment with different templates. Cut a small design or initial out of card and place it over a cookie. Dust the cookie with confectioners' sugar or cocoa before carefully removing the card.

Melting Chocolate

Melt chocolate slowly, as overheating will spoil both the flavor and texture. Dark chocolate should not be heated above 120°F; milk and white chocolate should not go above 110°F. Do not allow water or steam to come into contact with melting chocolate as this may cause it to stiffen. Leave chocolate uncovered after melting, as condensation could also cause it to stiffen.

Using a double boiler

1 Fill the bottom of a double boiler or saucepan about a quarter full. Fit the top pan or place a heatproof bowl over the saucepan. The water should not touch the top container. Bring the water to just below boiling point, then turn down the heat to the lowest possible setting.

2 Chop the chocolate or break it into squares and place in the top pan or bowl. Allow to melt completely. Stir until smooth. Keep the water at a very low simmer all the time.

▲ **Using the microwave** Chop the chocolate or break it into squares and place it in a bowl suitable for use in the microwave. Heat until just softened – chocolate burns easily in the microwave, so check often, remembering that chocolate retains its shape when melted in this way.

Approximate times for melting semisweet or milk chocolate in a 650–700 watt microwave oven are: 4 ounces, 2 minutes on High (100% power), 7–8 ounces 3 minutes on High (100% power), 4 ounces white chocolate, 2 minutes on Medium (50% power).

◀ **Using direct heat** This is only suitable for recipes where the chocolate is melted in plenty of other liquid, such as milk or cream. Chop the chocolate or break it into a saucepan. Add the liquid, then heat gently, stirring occasionally, until the chocolate has melted and the mixture is smooth.

Storing Cookies

Cookies should always be cooled completely before storing. When stored, crisp cookies tend to go soft, and soft ones can harden and dry out. The key to storing cookies is to choose an airtight container. This could be a jar or tin with a tight-fitting lid, or a rigid plastic box with a close-fitting lid. If you are not quite sure about the fit of a lid, put the cookies in a sealed plastic bag first. Alternatively, cover the top of the tin, jar or container with plastic wrap before putting on the lid.

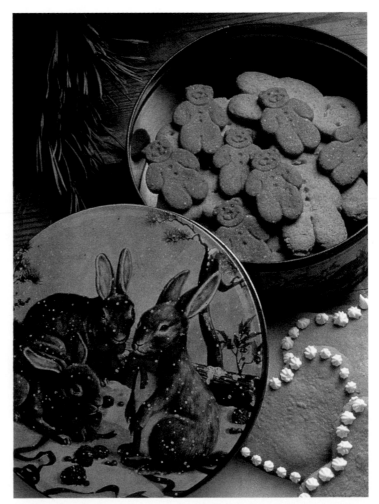

▲ **Glass jars** Glass jars with airtight stoppers or corks, or screw-topped lids, allow the cookies to be seen. Found mostly in kitchen departments or shops, some jars come in wonderful shapes and colors.

▶ **Tins** Tins make excellent airtight containers for cookies and come in all shapes and sizes. Look for the more unconventional shapes and designs in large stores, kitchen shops and stationers.

Gift-wrapping Cookies

Cookies make wonderful gifts, and you can easily make the wrapping as special as the contents for an irresistible present.

▶ **Gift-wrapping materials** The emphasis on attractive gift-wrap has increased considerably in recent years. It is relatively simple to make small gifts at home and package them beautifully. Personalized gifts are as much a joy to give as to receive.

There are many shops that specialize in gift-wrapping materials. Papers, ribbons, different types of boxes, containers, labels and cards are all available. When making your own gifts, look out for unusual accessories with which to enhance the packaging of the fruits of your labors. Keep an eye open for innovative containers in second-hand, collectible and antique shops and flea markets.

▲ **Boxes** These make wonderful containers for cookies. You will find many different designs, colors and sizes in stationers, paper specialists or large stores. If your gift will be given and eaten quickly, a pretty box lined with tissue paper may be the answer.

▲ **Bags** Paper and fabric bags can be used for cookies that are given and eaten quickly. They come in a variety of sizes and often have a matching gift label attached. A utilitarian brown paper bag undergoes a complete transformation when it is spatter-sprayed with gold and silver paint. Here it is decorated with a trio of candies wired to the ribbon and with gilded hydrangea heads stuck onto one side.

Cookie Tips & Techniques

▲ **Cellophane** For a simple yet stylish presentation, wrap neat piles of cookies in cellophane and tie with string or a pretty ribbon.

For a very special gift, choose a fine porcelain dish, cover with cellophane or clear wrap, and tie with a coordinating ribbon.

▲ Many different shapes and types of container make the gift seem that little bit extra special.

▶ **Gift cards and tags** These are often available to coordinate with your chosen paper, box or container. You can easily make your own tags by sticking your chosen paper onto a plain piece of card before making a hole in the corner and adding a ribbon. The choice of ribbons is overwhelming; even the simplest ribbons can transform a gift more than any other packaging.

Traditional Cookies

Snickerdoodles, Tollhouse Cookies, Melting Moments, Ginger Cookies, Scottish Shortbread – these are not just cookies but an integral part of a country's national cuisine, even its national heritage. Such cookies are foods we have known, eaten and loved all our lives, so making them can easily result in a trip along memory lane.

Traditional cookies have been made by generations of family and country cooks, usually using local produce, as in Brittany Butter Cookies, which come from the rich dairy land of western France, and Oatmeal Wedges from Scotland. The ingredients are inexpensive, available, everyday items and the methods straightforward.

Cookies will usually keep well; if they lose their freshness or crispness, they can be refreshed in a low oven, set at about 325°F for approximately three minutes.

It is a good idea to make a large batch of cookie dough and keep some in the freezer, either as a ball of dough, or ready-shaped, depending on the amount of room available, so you can quickly cook some cookies when you need them. Cookies can also be frozen after baking, but after defrosting will need to be refreshed in a low oven before serving.

Granola Cookies

Makes 18

INGREDIENTS

½ cup butter or margarine
½ cup light brown sugar
⅓ cup crunchy peanut butter
1 egg
½ cup all-purpose flour
½ teaspoon baking powder
½ teaspoon ground cinnamon
pinch of salt
2 cups granola
⅓ cup raisins
½ cup walnuts, chopped

1 Preheat the oven to 350°F. Grease a baking sheet. Put the butter or margarine in a bowl.

2 With an electric mixer, cream the butter or margarine and sugar until light and fluffy. Beat in the peanut butter, then beat in the egg.

3 Sift the flour, baking powder, cinnamon and salt over the peanut butter mixture and stir to blend. Stir in the granola, raisins and walnuts. Taste the mixture to see if it needs more sugar, as granolas vary in sweetness.

4 Drop rounded tablespoonfuls of the batter onto the prepared baking sheet about 1 inch apart. Press gently with the back of a spoon to spread each mound into a circle.

5 Bake for about 15 minutes, until lightly colored. With a metal spatula, transfer to a wire rack and allow to cool.

Crunchy Oatmeal Cookies

Makes 14

INGREDIENTS

¾ cup butter or margarine
¾ cup sugar
1 egg yolk
1½ cups all-purpose flour
1 teaspoon baking soda
pinch of salt
½ cup rolled oats
½ cup crunchy
nugget cereal

Variation For Nutty Oatmeal Cookies, substitute an equal quantity of chopped walnuts or pecans for the cereal, and prepare as described.

1 With an electric mixer, cream the butter or margarine and sugar together until light and fluffy. Mix in the egg yolk.

2 Sift over the flour, baking soda and salt, then stir into the butter mixture. Add the oats and cereal and stir to blend. Chill for at least 20 minutes.

3 Preheat the oven to 375°F. Grease a baking sheet. Flour the bottom of a glass.

4 Roll the dough into balls. Place them on the prepared baking sheet and flatten with the bottom of the glass.

5 Bake for 10–12 minutes, until golden. With a metal spatula, transfer to a wire rack to cool completely.

Coconut Oat Cookies

Makes 18

INGREDIENTS

2 cups quick-cooking oats
1 cup shredded coconut
1 cup butter or margarine, at
room temperature
$^1/_2$ cup granulated sugar
$^1/_4$ cup firmly packed dark brown
sugar
2 eggs
4 tablespoons milk
$1^1/_2$ teaspoons vanilla extract
1 cup all-purpose flour
$^1/_2$ teaspoon baking soda
pinch of salt
1 teaspoon ground cinnamon

1 Preheat the oven to 400°F. Lightly grease two baking sheets. Grease the bottom of a glass and dip in sugar.

2 Spread the oats and coconut on an ungreased baking sheet. Bake for 8–10 minutes, until golden brown, stirring occasionally.

3 With an electric mixer, cream the butter or margarine and both sugars until light and fluffy. Beat in the eggs, one at a time, then add the milk and vanilla extract. Sift over the dry ingredients and fold in. Stir in the oats and coconut.

4 Drop spoonfuls of the dough 1–2 inches apart on the baking sheets and flatten with the glass. Bake for 8–10 minutes. Transfer to a wire rack to cool.

Crunchy Jumbles

Makes 36

INGREDIENTS

$^1/_2$ cup butter or margarine, at
room temperature
1 cup sugar
1 egg
1 teaspoon vanilla extract
$1^1/_4$ cups all-purpose flour
$^1/_2$ teaspoon baking soda
pinch of salt
2 cups Rice Krispies
1 cup chocolate chips

Variation For even crunchier cookies, add $^1/_2$ cup walnuts, coarsely chopped, with the cereal and chocolate chips.

1 Preheat the oven to 350°F. Lightly grease two baking sheets.

2 With an electric mixer, cream the butter or margarine and sugar until light and fluffy. Beat in the egg and vanilla. Sift over the flour, baking soda and salt and fold in.

3 Add the cereal and chocolate chips. Stir to mix thoroughly.

4 Drop spoonfuls of the dough 1–2 inches apart on the prepared sheets. Bake for 10–12 minutes, until golden. Transfer to a wire rack to cool.

Malted Oat Crisps

These cookies are very crisp and crunchy – ideal to serve with morning coffee.

Makes 18

❧

INGREDIENTS

1 ½ cups rolled oats
¼ cup packed light brown sugar
1 egg
4 tablespoons sunflower oil
2 tablespoons malt extract

❧

1 Preheat the oven to 375°F. Lightly grease two baking sheets. Mix the rolled oats and brown sugar in a bowl, breaking up any lumps in the sugar. Add the egg, sunflower oil and malt extract, mix well, then let soak for 15 minutes.

2 Using a teaspoon, place small mounds of the mixture well apart on the prepared baking sheets. Press the mounds into 3-inch rounds with the back of a dampened fork.

3 Bake for 10–15 minutes, until golden brown. Allow to cool for 1 minute, then remove with a metal spatula and cool on a wire rack.

Variation To give these crisp cookies a fruity taste, add ½ cup chopped dates.

Shortbread

Makes 8

INGREDIENTS

²/₃ cup unsalted butter
¹/₂ cup sugar
1¹/₄ cups all-purpose flour
¹/₂ cup rice flour
¹/₄ teaspoon baking powder
pinch of salt

1 Preheat the oven to 325°F. Grease a shallow 8 inch cake tin.

2 With an electric mixer, cream the butter and sugar together until light and fluffy. Sift over the flours, baking powder and salt and mix well.

3 Press the dough neatly into the prepared tin, smoothing the surface with the back of a spoon. Prick all over with a fork, then score into eight equal wedges.

4 Bake for 40–45 minutes. Leave in the tin until cool enough to handle, then unmold and recut the wedges while still hot.

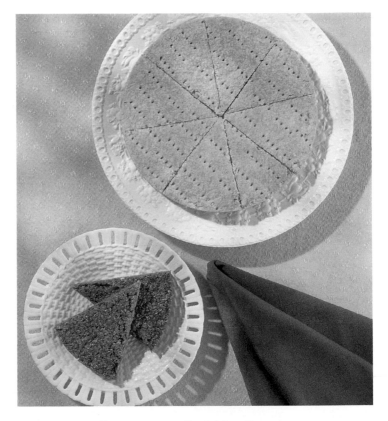

Oatmeal Wedges

Makes 8

INGREDIENTS

4 tablespoons butter
1¹/₂ tablespoons molasses
¹/₃ cup dark brown sugar
1¹/₄ cups rolled oats
pinch of salt

Variation If wished, add 1 teaspoon ground ginger to the melted butter.

1 Preheat the oven to 350°F. Line an 8 inch shallow cake tin with waxed paper and grease the paper.

2 Place the butter, molasses and sugar in a saucepan over a low heat. Cook, stirring, until melted and combined.

3 Remove from the heat and add the oats and salt. Stir to blend.

4 Spoon into the prepared cake tin and smooth the surface. Bake for 20–25 minutes until golden brown. Leave in the tin until cool enough to handle, then unmold and cut into eight equal wedges while still hot.

Melting Moments

These cookies are very crisp and light – and they melt in your mouth.

Makes 16–20

❧

INGREDIENTS

3 tablespoons butter or margarine
5 tablespoons lard or
vegetable shortening
¹/₂ cup sugar
¹/₂ egg, beaten
few drops of vanilla or
almond extract
1¹/₄ cups self-rising flour
rolled oats for coating
4–5 candied cherries, quartered

❧

1 Preheat the oven to 350°F. Grease two baking sheets. Cream together the butter or margarine, lard and sugar, then gradually beat in the egg and vanilla or almond extract.

2 Stir the flour into the beaten mixture, then roll into 16–20 small balls in your hands.

3 Spread the rolled oats on a sheet of waxed paper and toss the balls in them to coat evenly.

4 Place the balls, spaced slightly apart, on the prepared baking sheets, place a piece of cherry on top of each and bake for 15–20 minutes, until lightly browned. Allow the cookies to cool for a few minutes before transferring to a wire rack.

Apricot Yogurt Cookies

These soft cookies are very quick to make and are useful for lunch boxes.

Makes 16

🌿

INGREDIENTS

1 ½ cups all-purpose flour
1 teaspoon baking powder
1 teaspoon ground cinnamon
1 cup rolled oats
½ cup light brown sugar, plus
   some for sprinkling
¾ cup chopped ready-to-eat dried
   apricots
1 tablespoon slivered hazelnuts
   or almonds
⅔ cup plain yogurt
3 tablespoons sunflower oil

🌿

1 Preheat the oven to 375°F. Lightly oil a large baking sheet.

2 Sift together the flour, baking powder and cinnamon. Stir in the oats, sugar, apricots and nuts.

Cook's Tip These cookies do not keep well, so it is best to eat them within two days, or to freeze them. Pack into polythene bags and freeze for up to four months.

3 Beat together the yogurt and oil, then stir evenly into the flour mixture to make a firm dough. If necessary, add a little more yogurt. Use your hands to roll the mixture into about 16 small balls.

4 Place the balls on the prepared baking sheet and flatten with a fork. Sprinkle with light brown sugar. Bake for 15–20 minutes, until firm and golden brown. Transfer to a wire rack and leave to cool.

Applesauce Cookies

These fruit-flavored cookies are a favorite with children.

Makes 36

INGREDIENTS

*1 pound cooking apples, peeled,
cored and chopped
3 tablespoons water
¹/₂ cup sugar
¹/₂ cup butter or margarine
1 cup all-purpose flour
¹/₂ teaspoon baking powder
¹/₄ teaspoon baking soda
pinch of salt
¹/₂ teaspoon ground cinnamon
¹/₂ cup chopped walnuts*

1 Cook the apples with the water in a covered saucepan over low heat until the apple is tender. Cool slightly, then purée in a blender or mash with a fork. Measure out ³/₄ cup.

2 Preheat the oven to 375°F. Grease a baking sheet. In a medium-sized bowl, cream together the sugar and butter or margarine until well mixed. Beat in the applesauce.

Cook's Tip If the applesauce is too runny, put it in a strainer over a bowl and let it drain for 10 minutes before measuring it out.

3 Sift the flour, baking powder, baking soda, salt and cinnamon into the mixture, and stir to blend. Fold in the chopped walnuts.

4 Drop teaspoonfuls of the dough onto the prepared baking sheet, spacing them about 2 inches apart.

5 Bake the cookies for 8–10 minutes, until they are golden brown. Transfer to a wire rack and allow to cool.

Chocolate Chip Hazelnut Cookies

Chocolate chip cookies, with a delicious nutty flavor.

Makes 36

🌿

INGREDIENTS

1 cup all-purpose flour
1 teaspoon baking powder
pinch of salt
⅓ cup butter or margarine
1½ cups granulated sugar
⅓ cup light brown sugar
1 egg
1 teaspoon vanilla extract
⅔ cup chocolate chips
½ cup hazelnuts, chopped

🌿

1 Preheat the oven to 350°F. Grease 2–3 baking sheets. Sift the flour, baking powder and salt into a small bowl. Set aside.

2 With an electric mixer, cream together the butter or margarine and the sugars. Beat in the egg and vanilla extract. Add the flour mixture and beat well with the mixer on low speed.

3 Stir in the chocolate chips and half of the hazelnuts, using a wooden spoon.

4 Drop teaspoonfuls of the mixture onto the prepared baking sheets, to form ¾ inch mounds. Space the cookies 1–2 inches apart.

5 Flatten each cookie lightly with a wet fork. Sprinkle the remaining hazelnuts on top of the cookies and press lightly into the surface.

6 Bake for 10–12 minutes until golden. Transfer the biscuits to a wire rack and leave to cool.

Chocolate Chip Oat Cookies

Makes 60

❧

INGREDIENTS

1 cup all-purpose flour
¹/₂ teaspoon baking soda
¹/₄ teaspoon baking powder
pinch of salt
¹/₂ cup butter or margarine
¹/₂ cup granulated sugar
generous ¹/₂ cup firmly packed
light brown sugar
1 egg
¹/₂ teaspoon vanilla extract
³/₄ cup rolled oats
1 cup semisweet chocolate chips

❧

1 Preheat the oven to 350°F. Grease 3–4 baking sheets.

2 Sift the flour, baking soda, baking powder and salt into a mixing bowl. Set aside.

3 With an electric mixer, cream together the butter or margarine and the sugars. Add the egg and vanilla extract and beat until light and fluffy.

4 Add the flour mixture and beat on low speed until thoroughly blended. Stir in the rolled oats and chocolate chips. The dough should be crumbly. Drop heaped teaspoonfuls on to the prepared baking sheets, spacing the dough about 1 inch apart.

5 Bake for about 15 minutes, until just firm around the edge but still soft to the touch in the center. With a slotted spatula, transfer the cookies to a wire rack and allow to cool.

Mexican Almond Cookies

Light and crisp, these cookies are perfect with a cup of strong coffee.

Makes 24

❧

INGREDIENTS

1 cup all-purpose flour
1¹/₄ cups confectioners' sugar
pinch of salt
¹/₂ cup almonds, finely chopped
¹/₂ teaspoon vanilla extract
¹/₂ cup unsalted butter
confectioners' sugar for dusting

❧

Variation Try using other nuts such as walnuts, peanuts or pecans.

1 Preheat the oven to 350°F. Sift the flour, confectioners' sugar and salt into a bowl. Add the almonds and vanilla extract and mix well.

2 Using your fingertips, work the butter into the mixture to make a dough. Form it into a ball.

3 Roll out the dough on a lightly floured surface until it is ¹/₈ inch thick. Using a round cutter, stamp out into about 24 cookies, re-rolling the trimmings as necessary.

4 Transfer the cookies to nonstick baking sheets and bake for 30 minutes, until browned. Transfer to wire racks to cool, then dust thickly with confectioners' sugar.

Peanut Butter Cookies

For extra crunch, add ¹/₂ cup chopped peanuts with the peanut butter.

Makes 24

❧

INGREDIENTS

1 cup all-purpose flour
¹/₂ teaspoon baking soda
pinch of salt
¹/₂ cup butter
³/₄ cup firmly packed light brown sugar
1 egg
1 teaspoon vanilla extract
1 cup crunchy peanut butter

❧

1 Sift together the flour, baking soda and salt and set aside.

2 With an electric mixer, cream together the butter and sugar until light and fluffy.

3 In another bowl, mix the egg and vanilla extract, then gradually beat into the butter mixture.

4 Stir in the peanut butter and blend thoroughly. Stir in the dry ingredients. Chill for at least 30 minutes, until firm.

5 Preheat the oven to 350°F. Grease two baking sheets.

6 Spoon out rounded teaspoonfuls of the dough and roll into balls.

7 Place the balls on the prepared baking sheets and press flat with a fork into circles about 2¹/₂ inches in diameter, making a criss-cross pattern. Bake for 12–15 minutes, until lightly colored. Transfer to a wire rack to cool.

Tollhouse Cookies

Makes 24

❧

INGREDIENTS

¹/₂ cup butter or margarine
¹/₄ cup granulated sugar
¹/₂ cup firmly packed dark brown sugar
1 egg
¹/₂ teaspoon vanilla extract
1¹/₈ cups all-purpose flour
¹/₂ teaspoon baking soda
pinch of salt
1 cup chocolate chips
¹/₂ cup walnuts, chopped

❧

1 Preheat the oven to 350°F. Grease two baking sheets.

2 With an electric mixer, cream together the butter or margarine and the two sugars until the mixture is light and fluffy.

3 In another bowl, mix the egg and vanilla extract, then gradually beat into the butter mixture. Sift over the flour, baking soda and salt. Stir to blend.

4 Add the chocolate chips and walnuts, and mix to combine thoroughly.

5 Place heaping teaspoonfuls of the dough 2 inches apart on the prepared baking sheets. Bake for 10–15 minutes, until lightly colored. With a metal spatula, transfer to a wire rack to cool.

Snickerdoodles

Makes 30

INGREDIENTS

*½ cup butter
1½ cups sugar
1 teaspoon vanilla extract
2 eggs
¼ cup milk
3½ cups all-purpose flour
1 teaspoon baking soda
½ cup walnuts or pecans, finely
chopped
For the coating
5 tablespoons sugar
2 tablespoons ground cinnamon*

1 With an electric mixer, beat the butter until light and creamy. Add the sugar and vanilla extract and continue until fluffy. Beat in the eggs, then the milk.

2 Sift the flour and baking soda over the butter mixture and stir to blend. Stir in the nuts. Refrigerate for 15 minutes. Preheat the oven to 375°F. Grease two baking sheets.

3 To make the coating, mix the sugar and cinnamon. Roll tablespoonfuls of the dough into walnut-size balls. Roll the balls in the sugar mixture. You may need to work in batches.

4 Place the balls 2 inches apart on the prepared baking sheets and flatten slightly. Bake for about 10 minutes, until golden. Transfer to a wire rack to cool.

Chewy Chocolate Cookies

Makes 18

INGREDIENTS

*4 egg whites
2½ cups confectioners' sugar
1 cup cocoa powder
2 tablespoons all-purpose flour
1 teaspoon instant coffee powder
1 tablespoon water
1 cup walnuts, finely chopped*

1 Preheat the oven to 350°F. Line two baking sheets with waxed paper and then grease the paper well.

2 With an electric mixer, beat the egg whites until frothy.

3 Sift the sugar, cocoa, flour and coffee into the whites. Add the water and continue beating on low speed to blend, then on high for a few minutes, until the mixture thickens. With a rubber spatula, fold in the walnuts.

4 Place generous spoonfuls of the mixture 1 inch apart on the prepared baking sheets. Bake for 12–15 minutes, until firm and cracked on top but soft on the inside. With a metal spatula, transfer to a wire rack to cool.

Variation Add ½ cup chocolate chips to the dough with the chopped walnuts.

Buttermilk Cookies

Makes 15

🦋

INGREDIENTS

1¹/₂ cups all-purpose flour
pinch of salt
1 teaspoon baking powder
¹/₂ teaspoon baking soda
4 tablespoons cold butter or
margarine
³/₄ cup buttermilk

🦋

1 Preheat the oven to 425°F. Grease a baking sheet.

2 Sift the dry ingredients into a bowl. Rub in the butter or margarine until the mixture resembles coarse crumbs.

3 Gradually pour in the buttermilk, stirring with a fork until the mixture forms a soft dough.

4 Roll out to about ¹/₂ inch thick. Stamp out 2-inch circles with a cookie cutter.

5 Place on the prepared baking sheet and bake for 12–15 minutes, until golden. Serve warm or at room temperature.

Shortcake Cookies

These make a simple accompaniment to meals, or a snack with fruit preserves.

Makes 8

🦋

INGREDIENTS

1¹/₃ cups all-purpose flour
2 tablespoons sugar
1 tablespoon baking powder
pinch of salt
5 tablespoons cold butter, chopped
¹/₂ cup milk

🦋

Variation For Berry Shortcake, split the cookies in half while still warm. Butter one half, top with lightly sugared fresh berries, such as strawberries, raspberries or blueberries, and sandwich with the other half. Serve with dollops of whipped cream.

1 Preheat the oven to 425°F. Grease a baking sheet. Sift the flour, sugar, baking powder and salt into a bowl.

2 Rub in the butter until the mixture resembles coarse crumbs. Pour in the milk and stir with a fork to form a soft dough.

3 Roll out the dough to about ¹/₄ inch thick. Stamp out circles with a 2¹/₂-inch cookie cutter.

4 Place on the prepared baking sheet and bake for about 12 minutes, until golden. Serve these soft cookies hot or warm, spread with butter for meals. To accompany tea or coffee, serve with butter and jam or honey.

Traditional Sugar Cookies

Makes 36

❧

INGREDIENTS

3 cups all-purpose flour
1 teaspoon baking soda
2 teaspoons baking powder
¹/₂ teaspoon grated nutmeg
¹/₂ cup butter or margarine
1 cup sugar
¹/₂ teaspoon vanilla extract
1 egg
¹/₂ cup milk
colored or raw sugar for
sprinkling

❧

1 Sift the flour, baking soda, baking powder and nutmeg into a small bowl. Set aside.

2 With an electric mixer, cream together the butter or margarine, granulated sugar and vanilla extract until the mixture is light and fluffy. Add the egg and beat to mix well.

3 Add the flour mixture alternately with the milk to make a soft dough. Wrap in plastic wrap and chill for at least 30 minutes.

4 Preheat the oven to 350°F. Roll out the dough on a lightly floured surface to ¹/₈ inch thick. Cut into rounds or other shapes with floured cookie cutters.

5 Transfer to ungreased baking sheets. Sprinkle with colored or raw sugar. Bake for 10–12 minutes, until golden brown. Transfer the cookies to a wire rack to cool.

Brittany Butter Cookies

These little biscuits are similar to shortbread, but richer. Traditionally, they are made with lightly salted butter.

Makes 18–20

INGREDIENTS

6 egg yolks, lightly beaten
1 tablespoon milk
2¼ cups all-purpose flour
¾ cup sugar
scant 1 cup butter

1 Preheat the oven to 350°F. Butter a heavy baking sheet. Mix 1 tablespoon of the egg yolks with the milk to make a glaze.

2 Sift the flour into a bowl. Add the egg yolks, sugar and butter, and work them together until creamy.

3 Gradually bring in a little flour at a time until it forms a slightly sticky dough.

4 Using floured hands, pat out the dough to about ¼ inch thick and cut out rounds using a 3 inch cutter. Transfer the rounds to the prepared baking sheet, brush each with a little egg glaze, then, using the back of a knife, score with lines to create a lattice pattern.

5 Bake for about 12–15 minutes, until golden. Cool on the baking sheet on a wire rack for 15 minutes, then carefully remove the biscuits and leave to cool completely on the rack.

Cook's Tip To make a large Brittany Butter Cake, pat the dough with well-floured hands into a 9 inch loose-based cake pan or springform pan. Brush with egg glaze and score the lattice pattern on top. Bake for 45 minutes–1 hour, until firm to the touch and golden brown.

Toffee Cookies

Makes 36

❧

INGREDIENTS

¹⁄₄ cup unsalted butter, melted
1¹⁄₄ cups instant oatmeal
¹⁄₂ cup packed light brown sugar
¹⁄₂ cup dark corn syrup
2 tablespoons vanilla extract
large pinch of salt
³⁄₄ cup semisweet chocolate, grated
¹⁄₃ cup chopped walnuts

❧

1 Preheat the oven to 400°F. Grease a 15 x 10-inch baking pan.

2 Mix together the butter, oats, sugar, syrup, vanilla extract and salt and press into the prepared pan. Bake for about 15–18 minutes, until the mixture is brown and bubbly.

3 Remove from the oven and immediately sprinkle on the chocolate. Set aside for 10 minutes, then spread the chocolate over the base. Sprinkle on the nuts. Transfer to a wire rack to cool. Cut into squares.

Rose Water Thins

These light, crunchy cookies are easy to make and bake in minutes.

Makes 60

❧

INGREDIENTS

1 cup lightly salted butter
1 cup sugar, plus extra
for sprinkling
1 egg
1 tablespoon light cream
2¹⁄₂ cups all-purpose flour
pinch of salt
1 teaspoon baking powder
1 tablespoon rose water

❧

1 Preheat the oven to 375°F. Line two baking sheets with baking parchment.

2 Soften the butter and mix with all the other ingredients until you have a firm dough. Mold the mixture into an even roll and wrap in waxed paper. Chill until it is firm enough to slice very thinly. This will take 1–1¹⁄₂ hours.

3 Arrange the cookies on the prepared baking sheets with enough space for them to spread. Sprinkle with a little sugar and bake for about 10 minutes, until they are just turning brown at the edges.

Scottish Shortbread

Light, crisp shortbread looks very professional when shaped in a mold,
although you could also shape it by hand.

Makes 2 large or
8 individual shortbreads

INGREDIENTS

¼ cup all-purpose flour
¼ cup cornstarch
¼ cup sugar, plus extra for
sprinkling
½ cup unsalted butter, chopped

1 Preheat the oven to 325°F. Lightly flour the mold and line a baking sheet with baking parchment. Sift the flour, cornstarch and sugar into a mixing bowl. Rub the butter into the flour mixture until it binds together and you can knead it into a soft dough.

2 Place the dough into the mold and press to fit neatly. Invert the mold onto the baking sheet and tap firmly to release the dough shape. Bake for 35–40 minutes, until pale golden in color.

3 Sprinkle the top of the shortbread with a little sugar and cool on the baking sheet. Wrap in cellophane paper or place in a box tied with ribbon to make a delicious Christmas gift.

Spanish Churros

Makes 24

❦

INGREDIENTS

*1 cup water
1 tablespoon sugar, plus extra for
coating
pinch of salt
1¹/₂ cups all-purpose flour
1 egg
oil for deep frying
¹/₂ lime or lemon*

❦

Cook's Tip A funnel can be used to shape the churros. Close the end with a finger, add the batter, then release into the oil in small columns.

1 Bring the water, sugar and salt to a boil. Remove from the heat and beat in the flour until smooth.

2 Beat in the egg, using a wooden spoon, until the mixture is smooth and satiny. Set the batter aside.

3 Pour the oil into a deep frying pan to a depth of about 2 inches. Add the lime or lemon, then heat the oil to 375°F, until a cube of day old bread added to the oil browns in 30–60 seconds.

4 Pour the batter into a pastry bag fitted with a fluted nozzle. Pipe 3-inch strips of batter and then add to the oil, a few at a time. Fry for 3–4 minutes, until golden brown.

5 Using a slotted spoon, remove the churros from the pan and drain on paper towels. Roll the hot churros in sugar before serving with a cup of thick hot chocolate.

Golden Pillows

Makes 30

❦

INGREDIENTS

*2 cups all-purpose flour, sifted
1 tablespoon baking powder
pinch of salt
2 tablespoons lard, margarine or
vegetable shortening
³/₄ cup water
corn oil for frying
syrup or honey, to serve*

❦

Cook's Tip Use your imagination when deciding what to serve with the pillows. Sprinkle them with cinnamon and sugar, or syrup flavored with rum.

1 Put the flour, baking powder and salt into a large bowl. Lightly rub in the lard or margarine, using your fingertips, until the mixture resembles coarse breadcrumbs.

2 Gradually stir in the water, using a fork, until the mixture clings together to form a soft dough.

3 Shape the dough into a ball, then turn onto a lightly floured surface and knead very gently until smooth. Roll out thinly to a rectangle measuring about 18 x 15 inches. Using a sharp knife, carefully cut about thirty 3-inch squares. For a decorative edge, use a pastry wheel to cut out the squares.

4 Heat the oil to 375°F, until a cube of day old bread browns in 30–60 seconds.

5 Fry the squares, a few at a time, in the oil. As they brown and puff up, turn over to cook the other side. Remove with a slotted spoon and drain on paper towels. It is important that the temperature of the oil remains constant during the cooking process. Serve warm, with syrup or honey.

Chunky Chocolate Drops

Do not allow these cookies to cool completely on the baking sheet or they will become too crisp and will break when you try to lift them.

Makes 18

INGREDIENTS

6 ounces semisweet chocolate, chopped
¹/₂ cup unsalted butter, chopped
2 eggs
¹/₂ cup granulated sugar
¹/₃ cup light brown sugar
¹/₃ cup all-purpose flour
¹/₄ cup cocoa powder
1 teaspoon baking powder
2 teaspoons vanilla extract
pinch of salt
1 cup pecans, toasted and coarsely chopped
1 cup semisweet chocolate chips
4 ounces good-quality white chocolate, chopped into ¹/₄-inch pieces
¹/₂ cup good-quality milk chocolate, chopped into ¹/₄-inch pieces

1 Preheat the oven to 325°F. Grease two large baking sheets. In a medium saucepan over low heat, melt the semisweet chocolate and butter, stirring until smooth. Remove from the heat and set aside to cool slightly.

2 In a large mixing bowl, using an electric mixer, beat the eggs and sugars for 2–3 minutes, until pale and creamy. Gradually pour in the melted chocolate mixture, beating until well blended. Beat in the flour, cocoa powder, baking powder, vanilla extract and salt until just blended. Stir in the nuts, chocolate chips and white and milk chocolate pieces.

3 Drop heaping tablespoons of the mixture onto the prepared baking sheets 4 inches apart. Flatten each to 3-inch rounds. Bake for 8–10 minutes, until the tops are shiny and cracked and the edges look crisp; do not overbake or the cookies will become fragile.

4 Remove the baking sheets to a wire rack to cool for 2 minutes, then transfer cookies to the rack to cool.

Chocolate Marzipan Cookies

These crisp little cookies satisfy a sweet tooth and have a little almond surprise inside.

Makes 36

❧

INGREDIENTS

scant 1 cup unsalted butter
generous 1 cup light brown sugar
1 egg
2¹⁄₂ cups all-purpose flour
4 tablespoons cocoa powder
7 ounces white almond paste
4 ounces white chocolate, chopped

❧

1 Preheat the oven to 375°F. Lightly grease two large baking sheets. Cream the butter with the sugar in a bowl until pale and fluffy. Add the egg and beat well.

2 Sift the flour and cocoa over the mixture. Stir in, first with a wooden spoon, then with clean hands, pressing the mixture together to make a fairly soft dough.

3 Roll out about half the dough on a lightly floured surface to a thickness of about ¹⁄₄ inch. Using a 2 inch cookie cutter, cut out rounds, re-rolling the dough as required until you have about 36 rounds.

4 Cut the almond paste into about 36 equal pieces. Roll into balls, flatten slightly and place one on each round of dough. Roll out the remaining dough, cut out more rounds, then place on top of the almond paste. Press the dough edges to seal. Bake for 10–12 minutes until the cookies have risen well. Cool completely. Melt the white chocolate, spoon into a paper piping bag and pipe onto the biscuits.

Cook's Tip If the dough is too sticky to roll, chill it for about 30 minutes, then try again.

Double Chocolate Cookies

Keep these luscious treats under lock and key unless you're feeling generous.

Makes 18–20

❧

INGREDIENTS

¹/₂ cup unsalted butter
*²/₃ cup firmly packed light
brown sugar*
1 egg
1 teaspoon vanilla extract
1¹/₄ cups self-rising flour
³/₄ cup rolled oats
*4 ounces semisweet chocolate,
coarsely chopped*
*4 ounces white chocolate, coarsely
chopped*

❧

Cook's Tip If you're short of time when making the cookies, substitute chocolate chips for the chopped chocolate. Chopped crystallized ginger would make a delicious addition as well.

1 Preheat the oven to 375°F. Lightly grease two baking sheets. Cream the butter with the sugar in a bowl until pale and fluffy. Add the egg and vanilla extract and beat well.

2 Sift the flour over the mixture and fold in lightly with a metal spoon, then add the oats and chopped semisweet and white chocolate and stir until evenly mixed.

3 Place small spoonfuls of the mixture in 18–20 rocky mounds on the prepared baking sheets, leaving space for spreading.

4 Bake for 15–20 minutes, until beginning to turn pale golden. Cool for 2–3 minutes on the baking sheets, then transfer to wire racks to cool completely.

Chocolate and Nut Refrigerator Cookies

The dough must be chilled thoroughly before it can be sliced and baked.

Makes 50

❧

INGREDIENTS

2 cups all-purpose flour
pinch of salt
2 ounces semisweet chocolate,
chopped
1 cup unsalted butter
1 cup sugar
2 eggs
1 teaspoon vanilla extract
1 cup walnuts, finely chopped

❧

Variation For two-tone cookies, melt only 1 ounce chocolate. Combine all the ingredients, except the chocolate, as above. Divide the dough in half. Add the chocolate to one half. Roll out the plain dough on to a flat sheet. Roll out the chocolate dough, place on top of the plain dough and roll up. Wrap, slice and bake as described.

1 In a small bowl, sift together the flour and salt. Set aside. Melt the chocolate in the top of a double boiler, or in a heatproof bowl set over a saucepan of hot water. Set aside.

2 With an electric mixer, cream the butter until soft. Add the sugar and continue beating until the mixture is light and fluffy.

3 Mix the eggs with the vanilla extract, then gradually stir into the butter mixture.

4 Stir in the chocolate, then the flour followed by the nuts.

5 Divide the dough into four parts, and roll each into 2 inch diameter logs. Wrap tightly in foil and chill or freeze until firm.

6 Preheat the oven to 375°F. Grease two baking sheets. Cut the dough into ¼ inch slices. Place on the prepared sheets and bake for about 10 minutes. Transfer to wire racks to cool.

Chocolate Kisses

These rich little cookies look attractive mixed together on a plate and dusted with confectioners' sugar. Serve them with ice cream or simply with coffee.

Makes 24

INGREDIENTS

3 ounces semisweet chocolate, chopped
3 ounces white chocolate, chopped
1/2 cup butter
1/2 cup granulated sugar
2 eggs
2 cups all-purpose flour
confectioners' sugar, to decorate

1 Put each chocolate into a small bowl and melt it over a saucepan of hot, but not boiling, water, stirring until smooth. Set aside to cool.

2 Beat together the butter and granulated sugar until pale and fluffy. Beat in the eggs, one at a time.

3 Sift the flour over the butter, sugar and egg mixture and mix in thoroughly.

4 Halve the mixture and divide it between the two bowls of chocolate. Mix each chocolate in well. Knead the doughs until smooth, wrap them in plastic wrap and chill for 1 hour. Preheat the oven to 375°F. Grease two baking sheets.

5 Shape slightly rounded teaspoonfuls of both doughs roughly into balls. Roll the balls in the palms of your hands to make neater ball shapes. Arrange the balls on the prepared baking sheets and bake for 10–12 minutes. Dust with sifted confectioners' sugar and then transfer to a wire rack to cool.

Chocolate Pretzels

Makes 28

❦

INGREDIENTS

1 cup all-purpose flour
pinch of salt
3 tablespoons cocoa powder
¹/₂ cup butter
²/₃ cup sugar
1 egg
1 egg white, lightly beaten, for
glazing
sugar crystals for sprinkling

❦

1 Sift together the flour, salt and cocoa powder. Set aside. Grease two baking sheets.

2 With an electric mixer, cream the butter until light. Add the sugar and continue beating until light and fluffy. Beat in the egg. Add the dry ingredients and stir to blend. Gather the dough into a ball, wrap in waxed paper, and chill for 1 hour, or freeze for 30 minutes.

3 Roll the dough into 28 small balls. If the dough is sticky, flour your hands. Chill the balls until needed. Preheat the oven to 375°F.

4 Roll each ball into a rope about 10 inches long. With each rope, form a loop with the two ends facing you. Twist the ends and fold back on to the circle, pressing in to make a pretzel shape. Place on the prepared baking sheets.

5 Brush the pretzels with the egg white. Sprinkle sugar crystals over the tops and bake for 10–12 minutes until firm. Transfer to a wire rack to cool.

Chocolate, Maple and Walnut Swirls

Makes 12

INGREDIENTS

4 cups all-purpose flour
$\frac{1}{2}$ teaspoon ground cinnamon
4 tablespoons unsalted butter,
    chopped
$\frac{1}{4}$ cup granulated sugar
1 envelope easy-blend active
    dry yeast
1 egg yolk
$\frac{1}{2}$ cup water
4 tablespoons milk
3 tablespoons maple syrup,
    to finish
For the filling
3 tablespoons unsalted butter,
    melted
$\frac{1}{4}$ packed cup light brown sugar
1 cup semisweet chocolate chips
$\frac{3}{4}$ cup chopped walnuts

1 Grease a deep 9-inch springform cake pan. Sift the flour and cinnamon into a bowl, then rub in the butter until the mixture resembles coarse bread crumbs.

2 Stir in the sugar and yeast. In a cup, beat the egg yolk, with the water and milk, then stir into the dry ingredients to make a soft dough.

3 Knead until smooth, then roll out to about 16 x 12 inches. Brush with melted butter.

4 To make the filling, sprinkle the dough with the brown sugar, chocolate chips and chopped walnuts.

5 Roll up the dough from a long side like a jelly roll, then cut into 12 thick, even-sized slices.

6 Pack the slices closely together in the prepared cake pan. Cover and leave in a warm place for $1\frac{1}{2}$ hours, until well risen and springy to the touch. Preheat the oven to 425°F.

7 Bake for 30–35 minutes, until well risen, golden brown and firm. Remove from the pan and transfer to a wire rack. To finish, spoon the maple syrup over the cake. Pull the pieces apart to serve.

Cook's Tip The amount of liquid added to the dry ingredients may have to be adjusted slightly as some flours absorb more liquid than others.

Old-fashioned Ginger Cookies

Makes 60

❧

INGREDIENTS

2¹/₂ cups all-purpose flour
1 teaspoon baking soda
1¹/₂ teaspoons ground ginger
¹/₄ teaspoon ground cinnamon
¹/₄ teaspoon ground cloves
¹/₂ cup butter or margarine
1¹/₂ cups sugar
1 egg, beaten
4 tablespoons black molasses
1 teaspoon fresh lemon juice

❧

1 Preheat the oven to 325°F. Grease 3–4 baking trays.

2 Sift the flour, baking soda and spices into a small bowl. Set aside.

3 With an electric mixer, cream together the butter or margarine and two-thirds of the sugar.

4 Stir in the egg, molasses and lemon juice. Add the flour mixture and mix in thoroughly with a wooden spoon to make a soft dough.

5 Shape the dough into ³/₄ inch balls. Roll the balls in the remaining sugar and place them about 2 inches apart on the prepared baking trays.

6 Bake for about 12 minutes, until the biscuits are just firm to the touch. With a slotted spatula, transfer the biscuits to a wire rack and leave to cool.

Double Gingerbread Cookies

Packed in little bags or into a gingerbread box, these pretty cookies would make a lovely gift.

They are easy to make, but will have everyone wondering how you did it!

Makes 25

❦

INGREDIENTS

For the golden gingerbread
mixture
1¹/₂ cups all-purpose flour
¹/₄ teaspoon baking soda
pinch of salt
1 teaspoon ground cinnamon
¹/₃ cup unsalted butter, chopped
¹/₃ cup sugar
2 tablespoons maple or light
corn syrup
1 egg, beaten
For the chocolate gingerbread
mixture
1¹/₂ cups all-purpose flour
pinch of salt
2 teaspoons ground pumpkin
pie spice
¹/₂ teaspoon baking soda
4 tablespoons cocoa powder
¹/₃ cup unsalted butter, chopped
¹/₃ cup firmly packed light
brown sugar
1 egg, beaten

❦

1 To make the golden gingerbread,
sift together the flour, baking
soda, salt and spices. Rub the butter
into the flour in a large bowl, until
the mixture resembles fine
breadcrumbs. Add the sugar, syrup
and egg yolk and mix to a firm
dough. Knead lightly. Wrap in plastic
wrap and chill for 30 minutes
before shaping.

2 To make the chocolate
gingerbread, sift together the
flour, salt, spice, baking soda and
Knead the butter into the flour in a
large bowl. Add the sugar and egg and
mix to a firm dough. Knead lightly.
Wrap in plastic wrap and chill for at
least 30 minutes.

3 Roll out half of the chocolate
dough on a floured surface to an
11 x 1¹/₂-inch rectangle, ¹/₂ inch thick.
Repeat with half the golden
gingerbread dough. Using a knife, cut
both lengths into seven long, thin
strips. Lay the strips together, side by
side, alternating the colors.

4 Roll out the remaining golden
gingerbread dough with your
hands into a long sausage, ³/₄-inch
wide and the length of the strips. Lay
the sausage of dough down the center
of the striped dough.

5 Carefully bring the striped dough
up around the sausage and press
it gently into position to enclose the
sausage completely. Roll the
remaining chocolate dough into a
thin rectangle measuring
approximately 11 x 5 inches.

6 Bring the chocolate dough up
around the striped dough, to
enclose it. Press gently into place.
Wrap and chill for 30 minutes.

7 Preheat the oven to 350°F. Grease
a large baking sheet. Cut the
gingerbread roll into thin slices and
place them, slightly apart, on the
prepared baking sheet.

8 Bake for about 12–15 minutes,
until just beginning to color
around the edges. Leave on the
baking sheet for 3 minutes and
transfer to a wire rack to cool
completely.

Chocolate Cinnamon Tuiles

Makes 12

❧

INGREDIENTS

1 egg white
¼ cup superfine sugar
2 tablespoons all-purpose flour
3 tablespoons butter, melted
1 tablespoon cocoa powder
½ teaspoon ground cinnamon

❧

Cook's Tip Work as quickly as possible when removing the tuiles from the baking sheets – if they firm up too quickly, pop the baking sheet back in the oven for a minute and try again.

1 Preheat the oven to 400°F. Lightly grease two large baking sheets. Beat the egg white in a clean, grease-free bowl until it forms soft peaks. Gradually beat in the sugar to make a smooth, glossy mixture.

2 Sift the flour over the mixture and fold in evenly. Stir in the butter. Transfer about 3 tablespoons of the mixture to a small bowl and set aside.

3 In a separate bowl, mix together the cocoa and cinnamon. Stir into the egg white mixture.

4 Leaving room for spreading, drop spoonfuls of the chocolate-flavored mixture onto the prepared baking sheets, then spread each gently with a spatula to make a neat round.

5 Using a small spoon, drizzle the reserved plain mixture over the rounds to give a marbled effect.

6 Bake for 4–6 minutes, until just set. Using a metal spatula, lift each tuile carefully and quickly drape it over a rolling pin, to give a curved shape as it hardens.

7 Leave the tuiles to cool until set, then remove them gently and finish cooling on a wire rack. Serve on the same day.

Spiced-nut Palmiers

Makes 40

❧

INGREDIENTS

*²/₃ cup chopped
almonds, walnuts or hazelnuts
2 tablespoons sugar, plus extra
for sprinkling
¹/₂ teaspoon ground cinnamon
8 ounces rough-puff or puff
pastry, defrosted if frozen
1 egg, lightly beaten*

❧

1 Lightly butter two large baking sheets, preferably nonstick. In a food processor fitted with a metal blade, process the nuts, sugar and cinnamon until finely ground.

2 Sprinkle the work surface with sugar and roll out the pastry to a 20 x 8 inch rectangle about ¹/₈ inch thick. Brush the pastry lightly with beaten egg and sprinkle evenly with half of the nut mixture.

3 Fold in the long edges of the pastry to meet in the center and flatten with the rolling pin. Brush with egg and sprinkle with most of the nut mixture. Fold in the edges again to meet in the center, brush with egg and sprinkle with the remaining nut mixture. Fold one side of the pastry over the other.

4 Cut the pastry crossways into ³/₈ inch thick slices and place about 1 inch apart on the baking sheets.

5 Spread the pastry edges apart to form a wedge shape. Chill the palmiers for at least 15 minutes. Preheat the oven to 425°F.

6 Bake for about 8–10 minutes, until golden. Carefully turn them over halfway through the cooking time. Keep an eye on them as the sugar can easily scorch. Transfer to a wire rack to cool.

Cinnamon and Molasses Cookies

These cookies are slightly moist, spicy and nutty.

Makes 24

❧

INGREDIENTS

2 tablespoons black molasses
4 tablespoons butter or margarine
1 cup all-purpose flour
¼ teaspoon baking soda
½ teaspoon ground ginger
1 teaspoon ground cinnamon
1½ cups packed brown sugar
*1 tablespoon ground almonds or
hazelnuts*
1 egg yolk
1 cup confectioners' sugar, sifted

❧

1 Lightly grease a baking sheet. Heat the molasses and butter or margarine gently until just beginning to melt.

2 Sift the flour into a large bowl with the baking soda and spices, then stir in the sugar and almonds or hazelnuts.

3 Beat the molasses mixture and egg yolk briskly into the bowl, drawing the ingredients together to form a firm but soft dough.

4 Roll out the dough on a lightly floured surface to ¼-inch thick and stamp out shapes, such as stars, hearts or circles. Re-roll the trimmings and cut more shapes. Place on the prepared baking sheet and chill for 15 minutes.

5 Preheat the oven to 375°F. Prick the cookies lightly with a fork and bake for 12–15 minutes, until just firm. Transfer to wire racks to become crisp.

6 Mix the confectioners' sugar with a little lukewarm water to make it slightly runny, then drizzle it over the cookies on the wire racks.

Cinnamon Refrigerator Cookies

Makes 50

❧

INGREDIENTS

2 cups flour
pinch of salt
2 teaspoons ground cinnamon
1 cup unsalted butter
1 cup sugar
2 eggs
1 teaspoon vanilla extract

❧

1 In a bowl, sift together the flour, salt and cinnamon. Set aside

2 With an electric mixer, cream the butter until soft. Add the sugar and continue beating until the mixture is light and fluffy.

3 Beat together the eggs and vanilla extract, then gradually stir into the butter mixture.

4 Add the dry ingredients to the butter mixture and stir together until evenly combined.

5 Divide the dough into four parts, then roll each into 2 inch diameter logs. Wrap tightly in foil and chill or freeze until firm.

6 Preheat the oven to 375°F. Grease two baking sheets.

7 WIth a sharp knife, cut the dough into ¼ inch slices. Place the rounds on the prepared baking sheets and bake for about 10 minutes, until lightly colored. With a metal spatula, transfer to a wire rack to cool completely.

Spicy Pepper Cookies

Makes 48

❧

INGREDIENTS

1¾ cups all-purpose flour
½ cup cornstarch
2 teaspoons baking powder
½ teaspoon ground cardamom
½ teaspoon ground cinnamon
½ teaspoon grated nutmeg
½ teaspoon ground ginger
½ teaspoon ground allspice
pinch of salt
½ teaspoon freshly ground black
pepper
1 cup butter or margarine
1⅓ cups light brown sugar
½ teaspoon vanilla extract
1 teaspoon finely grated
lemon rind
¼ cup whipping cream
¾ cup finely ground almonds
2 tablespoons confectioners' sugar

❧

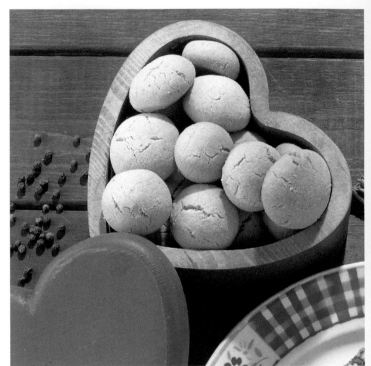

1 Preheat the oven to 350°F.

2 Sift the flour, cornstarch, baking powder, spices, salt and pepper into a bowl. Set aside.

3 With an electric mixer, cream the butter or margarine and brown sugar together until light and fluffy. Beat in the vanilla extract and grated lemon rind.

4 With the mixer on low speed, add the flour mixture alternately with the whipping cream, beginning and ending with flour. Stir in the ground almonds.

5 Shape the dough into ¾-inch balls. Place them on ungreased baking sheets, about 1 inch apart. Bake for 15–20 minutes, until golden brown underneath.

6 Allow to cool on the baking sheets for about 1 minute before transferring to a wire rack to cool completely. Before serving, sprinkle lightly with confectioners' sugar.

Lavender Heart Cookies

In folklore, lavender has always been linked with love, as has food, so make some heart-shaped cookies and serve them on Valentine's Day or any other romantic anniversary.

Makes 16–18

❧

INGREDIENTS

½ cup unsalted butter
¼ cup granulated sugar
1½ cups all-purpose flour
2 tablespoons fresh lavender
florets or 1 tablespoon dried
culinary lavender, roughly
chopped
2 tablespoons superfine sugar for
sprinkling

❧

1 Cream together the butter and sugar until fluffy. Stir in the flour and lavender and bring the mixture together in a soft ball. Cover and chill for 15 minutes.

2 Preheat the oven to 400°F. Roll out the dough on a lightly floured surface and stamp out about 18 cookies using a 2 inch heart-shaped cutter. Place on a heavy baking sheet and bake for about 10 minutes, until golden.

3 Sprinkle with sugar then leave the cookies standing for 5 minutes to set. Using a metal spatula, transfer carefully from the baking sheet onto a wire rack to cool completely. The cookies can be stored in an airtight container for up to one week.

Vanilla Crescents

These attractively shaped cookies are sweet and delicate, ideal for an elegant afternoon tea.

Makes 36

❧

INGREDIENTS

1¼ cups unblanched almonds
1 cup all-purpose flour
pinch of salt
1 cup unsalted butter
½ cup granulated sugar
1 teaspoon vanilla extract
confectioners' sugar for dusting

❧

1 Grind the almonds with a few tablespoons of the flour in a food processor, blender or nut grinder.

2 Sift the remaining flour with the salt into a bowl. Set aside.

3 With an electric mixer, cream together the butter and sugar until light and fluffy.

4 Add the almonds, vanilla extract and the flour mixture. Stir to mix well. Gather the dough into a ball, wrap in waxed paper, and chill for at least 30 minutes.

5 Preheat the oven to 325°F. Lightly grease two baking sheets.

6 Break off walnut-size pieces of dough and roll into small cylinders about ½ inch in diameter. Bend into small crescents and place on the prepared baking sheets.

7 Bake for about 20 minutes, until dry but not brown. Transfer to a wire rack to cool only slightly. Set the rack over a baking sheet and dust with an even layer of confectioners' sugar. Allow to cool completely.

Mexican Aniseed Cookies

Makes 24

❧

INGREDIENTS

1¹/₂ cups all-purpose flour
1 teaspoon baking powder
pinch of salt
¹/₂ cup unsalted butter
¹/₂ cup sugar
1 egg
1 teaspoon whole aniseed
1 tablespoon brandy
¹/₄ cup sugar mixed with
¹/₂ teaspoon ground cinnamon
for sprinkling

❧

1 Sift together the flour, baking powder and salt. Set aside.

2 Beat the butter with the sugar until soft and fluffy. Add the egg, aniseed and brandy and beat until incorporated. Fold in the dry ingredients until just blended to a dough. Chill for 30 minutes.

3 Preheat the oven to 350°F. Grease two baking sheets.

4 On a lightly floured surface, roll out the chilled dough to about ¹/₈ inch thick.

5 With a floured cutter, pastry wheel or knife, cut out the cookies into squares, diamonds or other shapes. The traditional shape for biscochitos is a fleur-de-lis but you might find this a bit too ambitious.

6 Place on the prepared baking sheets and sprinkle lightly with the cinnamon sugar.

7 Bake for about 10 minutes, until just barely golden. Cool on the baking sheet for 5 minutes before transferring to a wire rack to cool completely. The cookies can be kept in an airtight container for up to one week.

Festive and Fancy Cookies

Over the years, some cookies have become associated with certain festivals – Jeweled Christmas Trees dangle enticingly from the tree at Christmas, Easter Cookies always find their way into the cookie jar at that time of the year, and at carnival time Italians would feel deprived if Italian Pastry Twists did not make an appearance. Other cookies are festive just because they are fancy. Chocolate-Dipped Hazelnut Crescents or Black-and-White Ginger Florentines immediately perk up the spirits and make you feel something special is happening.

If you are making cookies for a holiday period such as school holidays, try to select recipes that keep well so you can make them a week or so in advance. Alternatively, freeze them, either raw or baked. Don't forget to make a note of how long they need to thaw, plus the baking time for raw cookies, and remember that cooked ones will benefit from being refreshed in the oven.

Baklava

This, the queen of all pastries, is enjoyed all year but is specially associated with many Greek holidays and festivities.

Makes 30

INGREDIENTS

3 cups ground pistachios
1¼ cups confectioners' sugar
1 tablespoon ground cardamom
⅔ cup unsalted butter, melted
1 pound filo pastry, defrosted
For the syrup
2 cups granulated sugar
1¼ cups water
2 tablespoons rose water

1 To make the syrup, place the sugar and water in a saucepan, bring to a boil and simmer for 10 minutes, until syrupy. Stir in the rose water. Mix together the nuts, confectioners' sugar and cardamom. Preheat the oven to 325°F. Brush a baking pan with butter.

2 Taking one sheet of filo pastry at a time, and keeping the remainder covered with a damp cloth, brush with melted butter and lay on the bottom of the pan. Continue until you have six buttered layers in the pan. Spread half of the nut mixture over, pressing down with a spoon.

3 Take another six sheets of filo pastry, brush with butter and lay over the nut mixture. Sprinkle over the remaining nuts and top with a final layer of six buttered filo sheets. Cut the pastry into small diamond shapes. Pour the remaining butter over the top. Bake for 20 minutes, then increase the heat to 400°F and bake for 15 minutes, until light golden in color and puffed.

4 Remove from the oven and drizzle most of the syrup over the pastry, reserving the remainder for serving.

Festive and Fancy Cookies

Almond Cinnamon Balls

These almond balls should be soft inside, with a very strong cinnamon flavor. They harden

with keeping, so it is a good idea to freeze some and thaw them when required.

Makes 15

❧

INGREDIENTS

1½ cups ground almonds
⅓ cup granulated sugar
1 tablespoon ground cinnamon
2 egg whites
oil for greasing
confectioners' sugar for dredging

❧

1 Preheat the oven to 350°F. Oil a large baking sheet. Mix together the ground almonds, sugar and cinnamon. Beat the egg whites until they begin to stiffen and fold enough into the almonds to make a fairly firm mixture.

3 Bake for about 15 minutes, so they remain slightly soft inside – too much cooking will make them hard and tough. Slide a metal spatula under the balls to release them from the baking sheet and allow to cool.

4 Sift a few tablespoons of confectioners' sugar onto a plate. When the cinnamon balls are cold, slide them onto the plate. Shake gently to completely cover the cinnamon balls in sugar. Store in an airtight container or in the freezer.

2 Wet your hands with cold water and roll small spoonfuls of the mixture into balls. Place these on the prepared baking sheet.

Coconut Pyramids

Coconut cookies are sold in Israeli street markets during Passover.

Makes 15

❧

INGREDIENTS

1 cup dried coconut
½ cup sugar
2 egg whites

❧

Cook's Tip The heat in ovens tends to be uneven, so, if necessary, turn the sheets around during baking for the pyramids to brown evenly.

1 Preheat the oven to 375°F. Grease a large baking sheet with a little oil.

2 Mix together the dried coconut and sugar. Lightly beat the egg whites. Fold enough egg white into the coconut to make a fairly firm mixture. You may not need all the egg whites.

3 Form the mixture into pyramid shapes by taking a teaspoonful and rolling it first into a ball. Flatten the base and press the top into a point. Arrange the pyramids on the prepared baking sheet.

4 Bake for 12–15 minutes on a low rack. The tips should begin to turn golden and the pyramids should be just firm, but still soft inside.

5 Slide a metal spatula under the pyramids and allow to cool before transferring to a wire rack.

Easter Cookies

These are enjoyed as a traditional part of the Christian festival of Easter.

Makes 16–18

❧

INGREDIENTS

½ cup butter, chopped
⅓ cup sugar, plus extra
for sprinkling
1 egg, separated
1¾ cups all-purpose flour
½ teaspoon pumpkin pie spice
½ teaspoon ground cinnamon
scant ⅓ cup currants
1 tablespoon chopped candied
citrus peel
1–2 tablespoons milk

❧

3 Turn the dough onto a floured surface, knead lightly until just smooth, then roll out using a floured rolling pin, to about ¼ inch thick. Cut the dough into rounds using a 2-inch fluted cookie cutter. Transfer the rounds to the prepared baking sheets and bake for 10 minutes.

4 Beat the egg white, then brush over the cookies. Sprinkle with sugar and return to the oven for another 10 minutes, until golden. Transfer to a wire rack to cool.

1 Preheat the oven to 400°F. Lightly grease two baking sheets. Beat together the butter and sugar, then beat in the egg yolk.

2 Sift the flour and spices over the egg mixture, then fold in with the currants and peel, adding sufficient milk to make a fairly soft dough.

Italian Pastry Twists

Deep-fried pastry twists, hearts or knots, traditionally flavored with vin santo, *a sweet Italian sherry, are served hot, dusted with confectioners' sugar, at Italian carnival time.*

Makes 40

INGREDIENTS

2¼ cups all-purpose flour
1 egg
pinch of salt
2 tablespoons granulated sugar
½ teaspoon vanilla extract
2 tablespoons butter, melted
3–4 tablespoons vin santo or
sweet sherry
oil for deep frying
confectioners' sugar for sprinkling

1 Sift the flour into a large mixing bowl and make a well in the center. Add the egg, salt, sugar, vanilla extract and melted butter.

2 Mix with your hands until the mixture starts to come together. When the dough becomes stiff, add enough sherry to make the dough soft and pliable. Knead until smooth and then wrap and chill for about 1 hour.

3 Roll out the pastry thinly and cut into 40 7 x ½-inch strips. Tie each strip loosely into a knot.

4 Heat the oil in a pan to 375°F and deep fry the knots in batches for 2–3 minutes, until puffed up and golden.

5 Drain the pastry twists on paper towels, sprinkle generously with confectioners' sugar and serve either hot or cold with coffee.

Apricot Meringue Bars

Makes 16

❧

INGREDIENTS

½ cup all-purpose flour
½ cup unsalted or lightly
salted butter
½ teaspoon vanilla extract
large pinch of salt
1 large egg, separated
⅓ cup sugar
⅓ cup chopped walnuts
⅓ cup chopped pecans
½ cup apricot preserves

❧

1 Preheat the oven to 350°F. Beat together the flour, butter, vanilla, salt, egg yolk, and ¼ cup of the sugar. Spread the mixture evenly over the base of a greased 8-inch baking pan, prick it all over with a fork and bake it in the oven for 10 minutes.

2 Beat the egg white until stiff. Gradually beat in the remaining ¼ cup of sugar until the mixture is smooth and glossy. Gently fold in the chopped walnuts and pecans, but do not over-mix.

3 Remove the pan from the oven, spread the apricot preserves over the base and spread the meringue mixture to cover it evenly.

4 Bake in the oven for 20 minutes, until the meringue is crisp and light brown. Cool on a wire rack, then cut into 4- x 1-inch bars for serving.

Cook's Tip Apricot Meringue Bars may be stored in an airtight container for up to 3 days.

Moravian Tarts

Makes 35

❧

INGREDIENTS

½ cup unsalted butter
½ teaspoon vanilla extract
large pinch of salt
scant ⅔ cup sugar
1 egg, beaten
1 cup all-purpose flour
¼ teaspoon baking soda
1½ teaspoons ground cinnamon
1 egg white, lightly beaten
35 pecan halves

❧

1 Cream the butter, vanilla extract, salt and ½ cup of the sugar until light and fluffy. Gradually add the egg, beating constantly.

2 Sift together the flour, baking soda and ½ teaspoon of the cinnamon and stir a little at a time into the butter mixture. Form the mixture into a dough and chill overnight. Remove from the refrigerator 30 minutes before using.

3 Preheat the oven to 350°F. Lightly grease a baking sheet. Roll out the dough until it is about ⅛ inch thick. Cut into rounds with a 2-inch cutter.

4 Place the rounds on the prepared baking sheet and brush the tops with the egg white. Mix the remaining ground cinnamon with the remaining sugar. Sprinkle over the rounds and press a pecan half into each center. Bake for 8–10 minutes, until golden brown.

Glazed Ginger Cookies

These also make good hanging cookies for decorating trees and garlands. For this, make a hole in each cookie with a skewer, when still warm, and thread with fine ribbon after it has cooked.

Makes about 20

❦

INGREDIENTS

*1 recipe Golden Gingerbread
mixture
2 recipes Icing Glaze
red and green food colorings
6 ounces white almond paste*

❦

1 Preheat the oven to 350°F. Grease a large baking sheet. Roll out the gingerbread dough on a floured surface and, using a selection of floured cookie cutters, cut out a variety of shapes, such as trees, stars, crescents and bells. Transfer to the prepared baking sheet and bake for 8–10 minutes, until just beginning to color around the edges. Leave the cookies on the baking sheet for 3 minutes.

2 Transfer the cookies to a wire rack and allow to cool. Place the wire rack over a large tray or plate. Using a teaspoon, spoon the icing glaze over the cookies until they are completely covered. Set aside in a cool place to dry for several hours.

3 Knead red food coloring into half of the almond paste and green into the other half. Roll a thin length of each colored paste and then twist the two together into a rope.

4 Secure a rope of paste around a cookie, dampening the icing with a little water, if necessary, to hold it in place. Repeat on about half of the cookies. Dilute a little of each food coloring with water. Using a fine paintbrush, paint festive decorations over the plain cookies. Allow to dry and then wrap in tissue paper.

Christmas Cookies

Makes 30

❦

INGREDIENTS

¾ cup unsalted butter
1¼ cups sugar
1 egg
1 egg yolk
1 teaspoon vanilla extract
grated rind of 1 lemon
pinch of salt
2½ cups all-purpose flour
For the decoration (optional)
colored icing and small candies
such as silver balls, colored sugar
crystals

❦

1 With an electric mixer, cream the butter until soft. Add the sugar gradually and continue beating until light and fluffy.

2 Using a wooden spoon, slowly mix in the whole egg and the egg yolk. Add the vanilla extract, lemon rind and salt. Stir to mix well.

3 Sift the flour over the mixture and stir to blend. Gather the dough into a ball, wrap, and chill for 30 minutes.

4 Preheat the oven to 375°F. On a floured surface, roll out the dough until about ⅛ inch thick.

5 Stamp out shapes or rounds with floured cookie cutters.

6 Bake for about 8 minutes, until lightly colored. Transfer to a wire rack and allow to cool completely before decorating, if wished, with icing and candies.

Jeweled Christmas Trees

These cookies make an appealing gift. They look wonderful hung on a
Christmas tree or in front of a window to catch the light.

Makes 12

🌿

INGREDIENTS

1½ cups all-purpose flour
⅓ cup butter, chopped
3 tablespoons sugar
1 egg white
2 tablespoons orange juice
8 ounces colored fruit candies
colored ribbons, to decorate

🌿

1 Preheat the oven to 350°F. Line two baking sheets with baking parchment. Sift the flour into a mixing bowl.

2 Rub the butter into the flour until the mixture resembles fine bread crumbs. Stir in the sugar, egg white and enough orange juice to form a soft dough. Knead on a lightly floured surface until smooth.

3 Roll out thinly and stamp out as many shapes as possible, using a floured Christmas tree cutter. Transfer the shapes to the prepared baking sheets, spacing them well apart. Knead the trimmings together.

4 Using a ½-inch round cutter or the end of a large plain pastry nozzle, stamp out and remove six rounds from each tree shape. Cut each candy into three and place a piece in each hole. Make a small hole at the top of each tree to thread through the ribbon.

5 Bake for 15–20 minutes, until the cookies are slightly golden in color and the candies have melted and filled the holes. Cool on the baking sheets. Repeat until you have used up the remaining cookie dough and candies. Thread short lengths of ribbon through the holes so that the cookies can be hung up.

Cranberry and Chocolate Squares

Made for each other – that's the contrasting flavors of tangy-sharp cranberries and sweet chocolate.

Makes 12

❦

INGREDIENTS

½ cup unsalted butter
4 tablespoons cocoa powder
1¼ cups firmly packed light
brown sugar
1¼ cups self-rising flour
2 eggs, beaten
1 cup fresh or thawed frozen
cranberries
For the topping
⅔ cup sour cream
6 tablespoons granulated sugar
2 tablespoons self-rising flour
4 tablespoons soft margarine
1 egg, beaten
½ teaspoon vanilla extract
5 tablespoons coarsely-grated
semisweet chocolate for sprinkling

❦

1 Preheat the oven to 350°F. Grease a 7 x 10 inch cake pan and dust lightly with flour. Combine the butter, cocoa and sugar in a saucepan and stir over low heat until melted and smooth.

2 Remove from the heat and stir in the flour and eggs. Stir in the cranberries, then spread the mixture in the prepared cake pan.

3 To make the topping, mix all the ingredients, except the chocolate, in a bowl. Beat until smooth, then spread over the base.

4 Sprinkle with the grated chocolate and bake for 40–45 minutes, until risen and firm. Cool in the pan, then cut into 12 squares.

Biscotti

These lovely Italian biscuits are part-baked, sliced to reveal a feast of mixed nuts and then baked again until crisp and golden. Traditionally they're served dipped in vin santo, *a sweet dessert wine.*

Makes 24

INGREDIENTS

¼ cup unsalted butter
½ cup sugar
1½ cups self-rising flour
pinch of salt
2 teaspoons baking powder
1 teaspoon ground coriander
finely grated rind of 1 lemon
½ cup medium yellow cornmeal
1 egg, lightly beaten
2 teaspoons brandy or orange-flavored liqueur
½ cup unblanched almonds
½ cup pistachios

1 Preheat the oven to 325°F. Lightly grease a baking sheet. Cream together the butter and sugar in a bowl.

2 Sift the flour, salt, baking powder and coriander into the bowl. Add the lemon rind, cornmeal, egg and brandy or liqueur and mix together to make a soft dough.

3 Stir in the nuts until evenly combined. Halve the mixture. Shape each half into a flat sausage about 9 inches long and 2½ inches wide. Bake for about 30 minutes, until risen and firm. Remove from the oven.

4 When cool, cut each sausage diagonally into 12 thin slices. Return to the baking sheet and cook for another 10 minutes, until crisp.

5 Transfer to a wire rack to cool completely. Store in an airtight container for up to one week.

Cook's Tip Use a sharp, serrated knife to slice the cooled biscotti, otherwise they will crumble.

Golden Raisin Cornmeal Cookies

These little yellow cookies come from the Veneto region of Italy.

Makes 48

❦

INGREDIENTS

½ cup golden raisins
1 cup finely ground yellow
cornmeal
1½ cups all-purpose flour
1½ teaspoons baking powder
pinch of salt
1 cup butter
1 cup sugar
2 eggs
1 tablespoon marsala or
1 teaspoon vanilla extract

❦

1 Soak the golden raisins in a small bowl of warm water for 15 minutes. Drain. Preheat the oven to 350°F. Grease a baking sheet.

2 Sift the cornmeal, flour, baking powder and salt together into a mixing bowl. Set aside.

3 Cream the butter and sugar until light and fluffy. Beat in the eggs, one at a time. Beat in the marsala or vanilla extract.

4 Add the dry ingredients to the butter mixture, beating until well blended. Stir in the golden raisins.

5 Drop heaping teaspoons of the mixture onto the prepared baking sheet in rows about 2 inches apart. Bake for 7–8 minutes, until the cookies are golden brown at the edges. Transfer to a wire rack to cool.

Amaretti

Almond extract will provide the flavor of bitter almonds, which are not available in the U.S.

Makes 36

❦

INGREDIENTS

1¾ cups almonds
flour for dusting
1 cup superfine sugar
2 egg whites
½ teaspoon almond extract or
1 teaspoon vanilla extract
confectioners' sugar for dusting

❦

1 Preheat the oven to 325°F. Peel the almonds by dropping them into a saucepan of boiling water for 1–2 minutes. Drain. Rub the almonds in a cloth to remove the skins.

2 Place the almonds on a baking sheet and let them dry out in the oven for 10–15 minutes without browning. Remove from the oven and allow to cool. Turn the oven off. Dust the almonds with flour.

3 Grind the almonds with half of the sugar in a food processor. Use an electric beater or wire whisk to beat the egg whites until they form soft peaks.

4 Sprinkle over half the remaining sugar and continue beating until stiff peaks are formed. Gently fold in the remaining sugar, the almond or vanilla extract and the almonds.

5 Spoon the almond mixture into a pastry bag fitted with a smooth nozzle. Pipe out the mixture in rounds the size of a walnut. Sprinkle lightly with the confectioners' sugar, and let stand for 2 hours. Near the end of this time, turn the oven on again and preheat to 350°F.

6 Bake for 15 minutes, until pale gold. Remove from the oven and cool on a wire rack.

Macaroons

Freshly ground almonds, lightly toasted beforehand to intensify the flavor,

give these macaroons their rich taste and texture so, for best results,

avoid using already-ground almonds as a shortcut.

Makes 12

INGREDIENTS

1½ cups blanched almonds,
toasted
¾ cup granulated sugar
2 egg whites
½ teaspoon almond or vanilla
extract
confectioners' sugar for dusting

1 Preheat the oven to 350°F. Line a large baking sheet with baking parchment. Reserve 12 almonds for decorating. In a food processor grind the rest of the almonds with the sugar.

2 With the machine running, slowly pour in enough of the egg whites to form a soft dough. Add the almond or vanilla extract and pulse to mix.

3 With moistened hands, shape the mixture into walnut-size balls and arrange on the baking sheet.

4 Press one of the reserved almonds onto each ball, flattening them slightly, and dust lightly with confectioners' sugar. Bake for about 10–12 minutes, until the tops are golden and feel slightly firm. Transfer to a wire rack, cool slightly, then peel the cookies off the paper and allow to cool completely.

Cook's Tip To toast the almonds, spread them on a baking sheet and bake in the preheated oven for 10–15 minutes, until golden. Allow to cool before grinding.

Madeleines

These little tea cakes, baked in a special pan with shell-shaped cups,

were made famous by Marcel Proust, whose great fiction starts off with

the taste of a madeleine.

Makes 12

INGREDIENTS

1¼ cups all-purpose flour
1 teaspoon baking powder
2 eggs
¾ cup confectioners' sugar, plus
extra for dusting
grated rind of 1 lemon or orange
1 tablespoon lemon or orange
juice
6 tablespoons unsalted butter,
melted and slightly cooled

1 Preheat the oven to 375°F. Generously butter a 12-cup madeleine pan. Sift together the flour and baking powder.

2 Using an electric mixer, beat the eggs and confectioners' sugar for 5–7 minutes, until thick and creamy and the mixture forms a ribbon when the beaters are lifted. Gently fold in the lemon or orange rind and juice.

3 Beginning with the flour mixture, alternately fold in the flour and melted butter in four batches. Allow the mixture to stand for 10 minutes, then carefully spoon into the pan. Tap gently to release any air bubbles.

4 Bake for 12–15 minutes, rotating the pan halfway through cooking, until a skewer or cake tester inserted in the center comes out clean. Turn onto a wire rack to cool and dust with confectioners' sugar before serving.

Cook's Tip If you don't have a special pan for making madeleines, you can use a muffin pan, preferably with a nonstick coating. The cakes won't have the characteristic ridges and shell shape, but they are quite pretty dusted with a little confectioners' sugar.

Chocolate Macaroons

Makes 20

〰

INGREDIENTS

*2 ounce semisweet chocolate
chopped into small pieces
1 cup blanched almonds
2 egg whites
1 cup superfine sugar
½ teaspoon vanilla extract
¼ teaspoon almond extract
confectioners' sugar for dusting*

〰

1 Preheat the oven to 300°F. Line two baking sheets with waxed paper and grease the paper.

2 Melt the chocolate in the top of a double boiler, or in a heatproof bowl set over a saucepan of barely simmering water.

3 Grind the almonds finely in a food processor, blender or nut grinder.

4 In a mixing bowl, whisk the egg whites until they form soft peaks. Then fold in the sugar, vanilla and almond extract, ground almonds and cooled melted chocolate. The mixture should just hold its shape. If it is too soft, chill for 15 minutes.

5 Place heaped teaspoonfuls of the mixture, spaced well apart, on the prepared baking sheets and flatten slightly. Brush each ball with a little water and sift over a thin layer of confectioners' sugar. Bake for 20-25 minutes, until just firm. With a metal spatula, transfer to a wire rack and allow to cool completely

Variation For Chocolate Pine Nut Macaroons, spread ¾ cup pine nuts in a shallow dish. Press the balls of chocolate macaroon dough into the nuts to cover one side and bake as described, nut-side up.

Coconut Macaroons

Makes 24

〰

INGREDIENTS

*⅓ cup all-purpose flour
pinch of salt
2½ cups dried coconut
⅔ cup sweetened condensed milk
1 teaspoon vanilla extract*

〰

1 Preheat the oven to 350°F. Line two baking sheets with waxed paper and grease the paper.

2 Sift the flour and salt into a large bowl. Stir in the dried coconut.

3 Pour in the sweetened condensed milk. Add the vanilla extract and stir together from the center. Continue stirring until a very thick batter is formed.

4 Drop heaping tablespoonfuls of batter 1 inch apart on the prepared baking sheets. Bake the macaroons for about 20 minutes, until golden brown. Transfer to a wire rack to cool.

Variation For a very rich, sweet and tempting petit four, make the macaroons smaller, and when cooked coat them in melted semisweet chocolate. Place on waxed paper and leave until the chocolate is hard. Serve with small cups of strong, black coffee after a dinner party.

Brandy Snaps

Celebrate with these on

holidays and happy days as

a special treat.

Makes 18

❧

INGREDIENTS

4 tablespoons butter
⅔ cup sugar
1 rounded tablespoon light
corn syrup
⅓ cup all-purpose flour
½ teaspoon ground ginger
For the filling
1 cup heavy or whipping cream
2 tablespoons brandy

❧

1 With an electric mixer, cream together the butter and sugar until light and fluffy, then beat in the light corn syrup. Sift over the flour and ginger and mix to a rough dough.

2 Transfer the dough to a work surface and knead until smooth. Cover and chill for 30 minutes.

3 Preheat the oven to 375°F. Grease a baking sheet.

4 Working in batches of four, form walnut-size balls of dough. Place well apart on the prepared baking sheet and flatten slightly. Bake for about 10 minutes, until golden.

5 Remove from the oven and allow to cool for a few moments. Working quickly, slide a metal spatula under each cookie, turn over, and wrap around the handle of a wooden spoon. When firm, slide off the snaps and place on a wire rack to cool.

6 To make the filling, whip the cream and brandy until soft peaks form. Fill a pastry bag and pipe into each end of the brandy snaps just before serving.

Chocolate-Dipped Hazelnut Crescents

Walnuts or pecans can be used instead of hazelnuts, but they must be finely ground.

Makes 35

INGREDIENTS

2½ cups all-purpose flour
pinch of salt
1 cup unsalted butter
¼ cup granulated sugar
1 tablespoon hazelnut liqueur
or water
1 teaspoon vanilla extract
3 ounces semisweet chocolate,
finely grated
½ cup hazelnuts, toasted and
finely chopped
confectioners' sugar for dusting
12 ounces semisweet chocolate,
melted, for dipping

1 Preheat the oven to 325°F. Grease two large baking sheets. Sift the flour and salt into a small bowl.

2 In a large bowl, using an electric mixer, beat the butter until creamy. Add the sugar and beat until fluffy, beat in the hazelnut liqueur or water and vanilla extract. Gently stir in the flour until just blended, then fold in the grated chocolate and hazelnuts.

3 With floured hands, shape the dough into 2 x ½ inch crescent shapes. Place on the prepared baking sheets, 2 inches apart. Bake for 20–25 minutes, until the edges are set and the cookies slightly golden. Remove the baking sheets to a wire rack to cool for 10 minutes. Transfer the crescents from the baking sheets to wire racks to cool completely.

4 Line the baking sheets with baking parchment. Dust the cookies with confectioners' sugar. Using a pair of kitchen tongs, or fingers, dip half of each crescent into melted chocolate. Place on the prepared baking sheets. Chill until the chocolate has set.

93

Black-and-White Ginger Florentines

These florentines can be refrigerated in an airtight container for one week.

Makes 30

❧

INGREDIENTS

½ cup heavy cream
¼ cup unsalted butter
½ cup sugar
2 tablespoons honey
1⅓ cups slivered almonds
⅓ cup all-purpose flour
½ teaspoon ground ginger
⅓ cup diced candied orange peel
½ cup diced crystallized ginger
7 ounces semisweet chocolate,
chopped
5 ounces good-quality white
chocolate, chopped

❧

3 Drop teaspoons of the mixture onto the prepared baking sheets at least 3 inches apart. Spread each round as thinly as possible with the back of the spoon. (Dip the spoon in water to prevent sticking.)

6 In a small saucepan over a very low heat, melt the remaining chocolate, stirring frequently, until smooth. Cool slightly. In the top of a double boiler over a low heat, melt the white chocolate until smooth, stirring frequently. Remove the top of the double boiler from the bottom and cool for about 5 minutes, stirring occasionally until slightly thickened.

1 Preheat the oven to 350°F. Lightly grease two large baking sheets. In a medium saucepan over medium heat, stir the cream, butter, sugar and honey until the sugar dissolves. Bring the mixture to a boil, stirring constantly.

2 Remove from the heat and stir in the almonds, flour and ground ginger until well blended. Stir in the orange peel, crystallized ginger and ⅓ cup chopped semisweet chocolate.

4 Bake in batches for 8–10 minutes, until the edges are golden brown and the cookies are bubbling. Do not underbake or they will be sticky, but be careful not to overbake as they burn easily. If you wish, use a 3-inch cookie cutter to neaten the edges of the florentines while on the baking sheet.

5 Remove the baking sheet to the wire rack to cool for 10 minutes until firm. Using a metal spatula, carefully transfer the florentines to a wire rack to cool completely.

7 Using a small metal spatula, spread half the florentines with the semisweet chocolate on the flat side of each cookie, swirling to create a decorative surface, and place on a wire rack, chocolate side up. Spread the remaining florentines with the melted white chocolate and place on the rack, chocolate side up. Chill for 10–15 minutes to set completely.

Tuiles d'Amandes

These cookies are named after the French roof tiles they so resemble. Making them can be difficult, so bake only four at a time until you get the knack. With a little practice you will find them easy.

Makes 24

❧

INGREDIENTS

*generous ½ cup whole blanched
almonds, lightly toasted
⅓ cup sugar
3 tablespoons unsalted butter
2 egg whites
½ teaspoon almond extract
scant ¼ cup all-purpose flour,
sifted
½ cup slivered almonds*

❧

Cook's Tip If the tuiles flatten or lose their crispness, reheat them on a baking sheet in a moderate oven until completely flat, then reshape.

1 Preheat the oven to 400°F. Generously butter two heavy baking sheets.

2 Place the almonds and about 2 tablespoons of the sugar in a food processor fitted with the metal blade and process until finely ground.

3 Beat the butter until creamy, then add the remaining sugar and beat until light and fluffy. Gradually beat in the egg whites, then add the almond extract. Sift the flour over the butter mixture, fold in, then fold in the ground almond mixture.

4 Drop tablespoonfuls of the mixture onto the prepared baking sheets about 6 inches apart. With the back of a wet spoon, spread each mound into a paper-thin 3 inch round. (Don't worry if holes appear, they will fill in.) Sprinkle with slivered almonds.

5 Bake the cookies, one sheet at a time, for 5–6 minutes, until the edges are golden and the centers still pale. Working quickly, use a thin spatula to loosen the edges of one cookie. Lift the cookie on the spatula and place over a rolling pin, then press down the sides of the cookie to curve it.

6 Continue shaping the cookies, transferring them to a wire rack as they cool. If they become too crisp to shape, return the baking sheet to the hot oven for 15–30 seconds, then continue as above.

Slivered Almond Cookies

Makes 30

❦

INGREDIENTS

¾ cup butter or margarine,
chopped
2 cups self-rising flour
⅔ cup sugar
½ teaspoon ground cinnamon
1 egg, separated
2 tablespoons cold water
½ cup slivered almonds

❦

3 Using a floured fluted round cutter, cut the dough into rounds. Use a metal spatula to lift them onto an ungreased baking sheet. Re-form the dough and cut more rounds to use all the dough. Beat the egg white lightly, brush it over the cookies, and sprinkle over the remaining sugar.

4 Bake for about 10–15 minutes, until golden. To remove, slide a metal spatula under the cookies, which will still seem a bit soft, but they harden as they cool. Let stand on a wire rack until quite cold.

1 Preheat the oven to 350°F. Rub the butter or margarine into the flour. Reserve 1 tablespoon of the sugar and mix the rest with the cinnamon. Stir into the flour and then add the egg yolk and cold water and mix to a firm dough.

2 Roll out the dough on a lightly floured board to ½ inch thick. Sprinkle over the almonds. Continue rolling until the dough is approximately ¼ inch thick.

Nut Lace Cookies

Makes 18

INGREDIENTS

½ cup blanched almonds
4 tablespoons butter
3 tablespoons all-purpose flour
½ cup sugar
2 tablespoons heavy cream
½ teaspoon vanilla extract

Variation Add ¼ cup finely chopped candied orange peel to the mixture.

1 Preheat the oven to 375°F. Grease 1–2 baking sheets.

2 With a sharp knife, chop the almonds as finely as possible. Alternatively, use a food processor, blender or nut grinder to chop the nuts very finely.

3 Melt the butter in a small saucepan over low heat. Remove from the heat and stir in the remaining ingredients, including the almonds.

4 Drop teaspoonfuls of the mixture 2½ inches apart on the prepared baking sheets. Bake for about 5 minutes, until golden. Cool on the sheets briefly, until the cookies are just stiff enough to lift off.

5 With a metal spatula, transfer the cookies to a wire rack to cool completely.

Oatmeal Lace Cookies

Makes 36

INGREDIENTS

⅔ cup butter or margarine
1½ cups rolled oats
¾ cup firmly packed dark brown sugar
¾ cup granulated sugar
3 tablespoons all-purpose flour
pinch of salt
1 egg, lightly beaten
1 teaspoon vanilla extract
½ cup pecans or walnuts, finely chopped

1 Preheat the oven to 350°F. Grease two baking sheets.

2 Melt the butter or margarine in a small saucepan over low heat. Set aside.

3 In a mixing bowl, combine the oats, brown sugar, granulated sugar, flour and salt.

4 Add the butter or margarine, the egg and vanilla extract.

5 Mix until blended, then stir in the chopped nuts.

6 Drop rounded teaspoonfuls of the batter about 2 inches apart on the prepared baking sheets. Bake for 5–8 minutes, until lightly browned on the edges and bubbling. Allow to cool for 2 minutes, then transfer to a wire rack to cool completely.

Strawberry Shortcakes

A favorite American summer dessert.

Makes 6

INGREDIENTS

*1 pound strawberries, hulled
and halved or quartered,
depending on size
3 tablespoons confectioners' sugar
1 cup heavy cream
mint leaves to decorate
For the shortcakes
2 cups all-purpose flour
⅓ cup superfine sugar
1 tablespoon baking powder
pinch of salt
1 cup heavy cream*

Cook's Tip To achieve the best results when whipping cream, chill the bowl and beaters until thoroughly cold. If using an electric mixer, increase the speed gradually, and turn the bowl while beating to incorporate as much air as possible.

1 Preheat the oven to 400°F. Lightly grease a baking sheet.

2 To make the shortcakes, sift the flour into a mixing bowl. Add ¼ cup of the superfine sugar, the baking powder and salt. Stir well.

3 Gradually add the cream, tossing lightly with a fork until the mixture forms clumps.

4 Gather the clumps together, but do not knead the dough. Shape the dough into a 6-inch log. Cut into six slices and place them on the prepared baking sheet.

5 Sprinkle with the remaining superfine sugar. Bake for about 15 minutes, until light golden brown. Allow to cool on a wire rack.

6 Meanwhile, mash a quarter of the strawberries with the confectioners' sugar. Stir in the remaining strawberries. Allow to stand for 1 hour at room temperature.

7 Just before serving, whip the cream until soft peaks form.

8 Slice each shortcake in half. Put the bottom halves on individual plates and top with some of the cream. Divide the strawberries among the six. Replace the tops and decorate with mint. Serve with the remaining cream.

Orange Shortbread Fingers

These are a real tea-time treat. The fingers will keep in an airtight container for up to 2 weeks.

Makes 18

❦

INGREDIENTS

½ cup unsalted butter
4 tablespoons sugar, plus extra
for sprinkling
finely grated rind of 2 oranges
1½ cups all-purpose flour

❦

1 Preheat the oven to 375°F.
Grease a large baking sheet.
Beat together the butter and sugar
until soft and creamy. Beat in the
orange rind.

2 Gradually add the flour and
gently pull the dough together to
form a soft ball. Roll out the dough
on a lightly floured surface to about
½ inch thick. Cut into fingers,
sprinkle over a little extra sugar and
put on the baking sheet. Prick the
fingers with a fork and bake for
about 20 minutes, until the fingers
are a light golden color.

Raspberry Sandwich Cookies

Children will love these sweet, sticky treats.

Makes 32

INGREDIENTS

1 cup blanched almonds
1½ cups all-purpose flour
¾ cup butter
½ cup sugar
grated rind of 1 lemon
1 teaspoon vanilla extract
1 egg white
pinch of salt
⅓ cup slivered almonds, chopped
1 cup raspberry jam
1 tablespoon lemon juice

1 Finely grind the blanched almonds and 3 tablespoons of the flour.

2 Cream together the butter and sugar until light and fluffy. Stir in the lemon rind and vanilla extract. Add the ground almonds and remaining flour and mix well to form a dough. Gather into a ball, wrap in waxed paper, and chill for 1 hour. Preheat the oven to 325°F. Line two baking sheets with waxed paper.

3 Divide the dough into four. Roll each piece out on a lightly floured surface to a thickness of ⅛ inch. With a floured 2½-inch pastry cutter, stamp out circles, then stamp out the centers from half the circles.

4 When all the dough has been used, make sure you have equal numbers of rings and circles, then place the dough rings and circles ½ inch apart on the prepared baking sheets.

5 Beat the egg white with the salt until just frothy. Brush only the cookie rings with the egg white, then sprinkle over the slivered almonds. Bake for 12–15 minutes, until very lightly browned. Allow to cool for a few minutes on the sheets before transferring to a wire rack.

6 In a saucepan, melt the jam with the lemon juice until it comes to a simmer. Brush the jam over the cookie circles and sandwich together with the rings. Store in an airtight container with sheets of waxed paper between the layers.

Pecan Tassies

These tiny sweet tarts accompany coffee perfectly.

Makes 24

❧

INGREDIENTS

½ cup cream cheese
½ cup butter
1 cup all-purpose flour
For the filling
2 eggs
⅔ cup packed dark brown sugar
1 teaspoon vanilla extract
pinch of salt
2 tablespoons butter, melted
1 cup pecan halves

❧

1 Place a baking sheet in the oven and preheat to 350°F. Grease 24 mini muffin pans.

2 Chop the cream cheese and butter. Put in a mixing bowl. Sift over the flour and mix to form a dough.

3 Roll out the dough thinly. With a floured fluted pastry cutter, stamp out 24 2½-inch rounds. Line the muffin pans with the rounds and chill.

4 To make the filling, lightly beat the eggs in a bowl. Gradually beat in the brown sugar, a few tablespoons at a time, and add the vanilla extract, salt and butter. Set aside until required.

5 Reserve 24 undamaged pecan halves and chop the rest coarsely with a sharp knife.

6 Place a spoonful of chopped nuts in each muffin pan and cover with the filling. Set a pecan half on the top of each.

7 Bake on the hot baking sheet for about 20 minutes, until puffed and set. Transfer to a wire rack to cool. Serve at room temperature.

Variation To make Jam Tassies, fill the cream cheese pastry shells with raspberry or blackberry jam, or other fruit jams. Bake as described.

Pecan Puffs

Makes 24

❧

INGREDIENTS

½ cup unsalted butter
2 tablespoons granulated sugar
pinch of salt
1 teaspoon vanilla extract
1 cup pecans
1 cup all-purpose flour, sifted
confectioners' sugar for dusting

❧

1 Preheat the oven to 300°F. Grease two baking sheets.

2 Cream the butter and sugar until light and fluffy. Stir in the salt and vanilla extract.

3 Grind the nuts in a food processor or nut grinder. Stir several times to prevent nuts from becoming oily.

4 Push the ground nuts through a sieve set over a bowl to aerate them. Pieces too large to go through the sieve can be ground again.

5 Stir the nuts and flour into the butter mixture to make a dough. Roll the dough into marble-size balls between the palms of your hands. Place on the prepared baking sheets and bake for 45 minutes.

6 While the puffs are still hot, roll them in confectioners' sugar. Leave to cool completely, then roll once more in confectioners' sugar.

Sablés with Goat Cheese and Strawberries

Sablés are little French cookies, made from egg yolk and butter. Crisp and slightly sweet,
they contrast perfectly with the tangy goat cheese and juicy strawberries.

Makes 24

INGREDIENTS

⅓ cup butter
1¼ cups all-purpose flour
¾ cup blanched hazelnuts, lightly
toasted and ground
2 tablespoons sugar
2 egg yolks, beaten with
2–3 tablespoons water
4 ounces goat cheese
4–6 large strawberries, cut into
small pieces
hazelnuts and mint, to decorate

1 Put the butter, flour, ground hazelnuts, sugar and beaten egg yolks into a food processor and process to a smooth dough. Scrape out the dough. Shape into a log about 1½ inch thick. Wrap and chill.

2 Preheat the oven to 400°F. Line a large baking sheet with baking parchment. With a sharp knife, slice the dough into ¼ inch thick rounds and arrange on the prepared baking sheet. Bake for 7–10 minutes, until golden brown. Transfer to a wire rack to cool and crisp slightly.

3 On a plate, crumble the goat cheese into small pieces. Mound a little goat cheese onto each sablé, top with a piece of strawberry and sprinkle with a few hazelnuts and mint leaves. Serve warm.

Variation These sablés are ideal served with fruit. Beat ⅓ cup cream cheese with 1 tablespoon confectioners' sugar and a little lemon or orange rind. Spread a little on the sablés and top with a few pieces of sliced kiwi fruit, peach, nectarine and a few raspberries.

Coffee Sponge Drops

These are delicious on their own, but taste even better with a filling
of low-fat cream cheese and chopped crystallized ginger.

Makes 12

INGREDIENTS

½ cup all-purpose flour
1 tablespoon instant coffee
powder
2 eggs
⅓ cup sugar
For the filling
½ cup low-fat cream cheese
¼ cup chopped crystallized ginger

1 Preheat the oven to 375°F. Sift the flour and instant coffee powder together. To make the filling, beat together the cream cheese and crystallized ginger. Chill until required.

2 Combine the eggs and sugar. Beat with an electric mixer until thick and mousse-like.

3 Carefully add the sifted flour and coffee to the egg mixture and gently fold in with a metal spoon, being careful not to knock out any air.

4 Spoon the mixture into a pastry bag fitted with a ½-inch plain nozzle. Pipe 1½-inch rounds on to lined baking sheets. Bake for 12 minutes. Cool on a wire rack. Sandwich together with the filling.

Ladyfingers

Named after the pale, slim fingers of fairy-tale princesses.

Makes 18

INGREDIENTS

⅔ cup all-purpose flour
pinch of salt
4 eggs, separated
½ cup granulated sugar
½ teaspoon vanilla extract
confectioners' sugar for sprinkling

1 Preheat the oven to 300°F. Grease two baking sheets, then coat lightly with flour, and shake off the excess.

2 Sift the flour and salt together two times.

3 With an electric mixer, beat the egg yolks with half of the sugar until thick enough to leave a ribbon trail when the beaters are lifted.

4 In another bowl, beat the egg whites until stiff. Beat in the remaining sugar until glossy.

5 Sift the flour over the yolks and spoon a large dollop of egg whites over the flour. Carefully fold in with a large metal spoon, adding the vanilla extract. Gently fold in the remaining whites.

6 Spoon the mixture into a pastry bag fitted with a plain nozzle. Pipe 4-inch long lines on the prepared baking sheets about 1 inch apart. Sift over a layer of confectioners' sugar. Turn the sheet upside down to dislodge any excess sugar.

7 Bake for about 20 minutes, until crusty on the outside but soft in the center. Cool slightly on the baking sheets before transferring to a wire rack.

Walnut Cookies

Makes 60

INGREDIENTS

½ cup butter or margarine
¾ cup sugar
1 cup all-purpose flour
2 teaspoons vanilla extract
1 cup walnuts, finely chopped

1 Preheat the oven to 300°F. Grease two baking sheets.

2 With an electric mixer, cream the butter or margarine until soft. Add ¼ cup of the sugar and continue beating until light and fluffy. Stir in the flour, vanilla extract and walnuts. Drop teaspoonfuls of the batter 1–2 inches apart on the prepared baking sheets and flatten slightly. Bake for about 25 minutes.

3 Transfer to a wire rack set over a baking sheet and sprinkle with the remaining sugar.

Variation To make Almond Cookies, use an equal amount of finely chopped unblanched almonds instead of walnuts. Replace half the vanilla with ½ teaspoon almond extract.

Mocha Viennese Swirls

Makes 20

❧

INGREDIENTS

9 ounces semisweet chocolate,
chopped
scant 1 cup unsalted butter
½ cup confectioners' sugar
2 tablespoons strong black coffee
1¾ cups all-purpose flour
½ cup cornstarch
about 20 blanched almonds

❧

Cook's Tip If the mixture is too stiff
to pipe, soften it with a little more
black coffee.

1 Preheat the oven to 375°F.
Lightly grease two large baking
sheets. Melt 4 ounces of the chocolate
in a heatproof bowl over a saucepan
of hot water. Cream the butter with
the confectioners' sugar in a bowl
until smooth and pale. Beat in the
melted chocolate, then the strong
black coffee.

2 Sift the flour and cornstarch over
the mixture. Fold in lightly and
evenly to make a soft mixture.

3 Spoon the mixture into a piping
bag fitted with a large star nozzle
and pipe 20 swirls on the prepared
baking sheets, allowing room for
spreading during baking.

4 Press an almond into the center
of each swirl. Bake for about
15 minutes, until the cookies are firm
and just beginning to brown. Allow
to cool for about 10 minutes on the
baking sheets, then lift carefully on
to a wire rack to cool completely.

5 Melt the remaining chocolate and
dip the base of each swirl to coat.
Place on a sheet of baking parchment
and allow to set.

Chocolate Amaretti

Makes 24

❧

INGREDIENTS

1¼ cups blanched whole almonds
scant ½ cup superfine sugar
1 tablespoon cocoa powder
2 tablespoons confectioners' sugar
2 egg whites
pinch of cream of tartar
1 teaspoon almond extract
slivered almonds, to decorate

❧

1 Preheat the oven to 350°F. Place the blanched almonds on a baking sheet and bake for 10–12 minutes, until golden brown. Set aside to cool. Reduce the oven temperature to 325°F. Line a large baking sheet with baking parchment. In a food processor, process the almonds with half the superfine sugar until they are finely ground, but not oily. Transfer to a bowl and sift in the cocoa and confectioners' sugar. Set aside.

2 In a mixing bowl with an electric mixer, beat the egg whites and cream of tartar until stiff peaks form. Sprinkle in the remaining superfine sugar a tablespoon at a time, beating well after each addition, and continue beating until the whites are glossy and stiff. Beat in the almond extract.

3 Sprinkle over the almond-sugar mixture and gently fold into the beaten egg whites until just blended. Spoon the mixture into a large pastry bag fitted with a plain ½-inch nozzle. Pipe 1½-inch rounds about 1 inch apart on the prepared baking sheet. Press a slivered almond into the center of each.

4 Bake the cookies for 12–15 minutes, or until crisp. Remove the baking sheets to a wire rack to cool for 10 minutes. With a metal spatula, remove the amaretti to a wire rack to cool completely.

Decorated Chocolate Lebkuchen

Wrapped in paper or cellophane, or beautifully boxed, these decorated cookies make a lovely present. Don't make them too far in advance as the chocolate will gradually discolor.

Makes 40

❦

INGREDIENTS

1 recipe Lebkuchen mixture
4 ounces semisweet chocolate, chopped
4 ounces milk chocolate, chopped
4 ounces white chocolate, chopped
chocolate sprinkles, for sprinkling
cocoa powder or confectioners' sugar for dusting

❦

1 Grease two baking sheets. Roll out just over half of the Lebkuchen mixture until ¼ inch thick. Cut out heart shapes, using a 1¾-inch heart-shaped cutter. Transfer to the baking sheets. Gather the trimmings together with the remaining dough and cut into 20 pieces. Roll into balls and place on the baking sheet. Flatten each ball slightly with your fingers.

2 Chill both sheets for 30 minutes. Preheat the oven to 350°F. Bake for 8–10 minutes. Cool on a wire rack.

3 Melt the semisweet chocolate in a heatproof bowl over a small saucepan of hot water. Melt the milk and white chocolate in separate bowls.

4 Make three small paper pastry bags out of waxed paper. Spoon a little of each chocolate into the three paper pastry bags and reserve. Spoon a little semisweet chocolate over one third of the cookies, spreading it slightly to cover them completely. (Tapping the rack gently will help the chocolate to run down the sides.)

5 Snip the merest tip from the bag of white chocolate and drizzle it over some of the coated biscuits, to give a decorative finish.

6 Sprinkle the chocolate sprinkles over the semisweet chocolate-coated cookies that haven't been decorated. Coat the remaining cookies with the milk and white chocolate and decorate some of these with more chocolate from the piping bags, contrasting the colors. Scatter more undecorated cookies with chocolate sprinkles. Allow the cookies to set.

7 Transfer the undecorated cookies to a plate or tray and dust with cocoa powder or confectioners' sugar.

Cook's Tip If the chocolate in the bowls starts to set before you have finished decorating, put the bowls back over the heat for 1–2 minutes. If the chocolate in the pastry bags starts to harden, microwave briefly or put in a clean bowl over a pan of simmering water until soft.

Fruit and Nut Lebkuchen

These simple, chunky gingerbread cookies make a delicious gift, especially when presented in a decorative gift box. The combination of walnuts, almonds and cherries is very effective, but you can use any other mixture of candied fruits and nuts.

Makes 20

INGREDIENTS

4 tablespoons granulated sugar
⅓ cup water
8 ounces semisweet chocolate, chopped
¾ cup walnut halves
⅓ cup candied cherries, chopped into small wedges
1 cup whole blanched almonds
For the Lebkuchen
½ cup unsalted butter
⅔ cup firmly packed light brown sugar
1 egg, beaten
⅓ cup molasses
3½ cups self-rising flour
1 teaspoon ground ginger
½ teaspoon ground cloves
¼ teaspoon cayenne pepper

Cook's Tip Carefully stack the cookies in a pretty box or tin, lined with tissue paper, or tie in cellophane bundles.

1 To make the Lebkuchen, cream together the butter and sugar until pale and fluffy. Beat in the egg and molasses. Sift the flour, ginger, cloves and cayenne pepper into the bowl. Using a wooden spoon, gradually mix the ingredients together to make a stiff paste. Turn onto a lightly floured work surface and knead lightly until smooth. Wrap and chill for 30 minutes.

2 Preheat the oven to 350°F. Grease two baking sheets. Shape the dough into a roll, 8 inches long. Chill for 30 minutes. Cut into 20 slices and space them on the baking sheets. Bake for 10 minutes. Leave on the baking sheets for 5 minutes and then transfer to a wire rack and set aside to cool.

3 Put the sugar and water in a small, heavy-bottomed saucepan. Heat gently until the sugar dissolves. Bring to a boil and boil for 1 minute, until slightly syrupy. Leave for 3 minutes, to cool slightly, and then stir in the chocolate until it has melted and made a smooth sauce.

4 Place the wire rack of cookies over a large tray or board. Spoon a little of the chocolate mixture over the cookies, spreading it to the edges with the back of the spoon.

5 Gently press a walnut half into the center of each cookie. Arrange pieces of candied cherry and almonds alternately around the nuts. Allow to set in a cool place.

Chocolate Almond Torrone

Serve this Italian speciality in thin slices.

Makes 20

❦

INGREDIENTS

*4 ounces semisweet chocolate,
chopped
4 tablespoons unsalted butter
1 egg white
½ cup superfine sugar
½ cup ground almonds
¾ cup chopped almonds, toasted
5 tablespoons chopped candied peel
For the coating
6 ounces white chocolate, chopped
2 tablespoons unsalted butter
1 cup slivered almonds, toasted*

❦

1 Melt the chocolate with the butter in a heatproof bowl over a saucepan of hot water, stirring until the mixture is smooth.

2 In a clean, grease-free bowl, beat the egg white with the sugar until stiff. Gradually beat in the melted chocolate, then stir in the ground almonds, chopped toasted almonds and chopped peel.

3 Tip the mixture onto a large sheet of baking parchment and shape into a thick roll.

4 As the mixture cools, use the paper to press the roll firmly into a triangular shape. Twist the paper over the triangular roll and chill until completely set.

5 To make the coating, melt the white chocolate with the butter in a heatproof bowl over a saucepan of hot water. Unwrap the chocolate roll and spread the white chocolate quickly over the surface. Press the slivered almonds in a thin, even coat over the chocolate, working quickly before the chocolate sets.

6 Chill again until firm, then cut the torrone into fairly thin slices to serve.

Cook's Tip The mixture can be shaped into a simple round roll instead of the triangular shape if you prefer.

Chocolate Hazelnut Galettes

*There's stacks of sophistication in these triple-tiered chocolate rounds
sandwiched with a light fromage blanc filling.*

Makes 4

◐

INGREDIENTS

*6 ounces semisweet chocolate,
chopped
3 tablespoons light cream
2 tablespoons slivered hazelnuts
4 ounces white chocolate, chopped
¾ cup fromage blanc
1 tablespoon dry sherry
4 tablespoons finely chopped
hazelnuts, toasted
physalis (Cape gooseberries),
dipped in white chocolate,
to decorate*

◐

1 Melt the semisweet chocolate in a
heatproof bowl over a saucepan
of hot water, then remove from the
heat and stir in the cream.

2 Draw 12 3-inch circles on sheets
of baking parchment. Turn the
paper over and spread the semisweet
chocolate over each marked circle,
covering in a thin, even layer. Scatter
slivered hazelnuts over four of the
circles, then put aside until set.

3 Melt the white chocolate in a
heatproof bowl over a saucepan
of hot water, then stir in the fromage
blanc and dry sherry. Fold in the
chopped, toasted hazelnuts. Allow to
cool until the mixture holds its shape.

Cook's Tip If gooseberries aren't
available, raspberries or blackberries
make delicious substitutes.

4 Remove the semisweet chocolate
rounds carefully from the paper
and sandwich them together in stacks
of 3, spooning the white chocolate
hazelnut cream between each layer
and using the hazelnut-covered
rounds on top. Chill before serving.

5 To serve, place the galettes on
individual plates and decorate
with chocolate-dipped physalis.

Savory
Treats

The earliest cookies were savory, made with just flour, water and perhaps some salt, but as the practice of cookie-making became established the savory version lost ground to sweet cookies. Now, there is a trend toward more savory tastes with more wine being drunk, and quaffed more casually rather than consumed only as an accompaniment to special meals, so savory cookies, often called biscuits, are making a comeback. This time, though, the recipes are far more varied and appetizing. Variety is introduced by using different flours, and including ingredients such as oats, cornmeal and nuts for texture. Savory cookie doughs are flavored with cheese, herbs and spices, or topped with sesame or other seeds for extra crunch and savor.

Try sandwiching savory cookies together in pairs with soft cheese, simply seasoned or flavored with a complementary ingredient, such as chives with cheese biscuits. Triple-deckers can be created in the same way. Avoid filling cookies too far in advance, though, in case they soften.

Any type of savory cookie is versatile — it can be served with drinks, soups and cheese, or taken in packed lunches and picnics.

Festive Nibbles

Shape these spicy cheese snacks in any way you wish –

stars, crescent moons, triangles, squares, hearts,

fingers or rounds. Serve them with drinks from

ice-cold cocktails to hot and spicy mulled wine and spirits.

Makes 60

❧

INGREDIENTS

*1 cup all-purpose flour, plus extra
for dusting
1 teaspoon dry mustard
pinch of salt
¹/₂ cup butter
¹/₄ cup Cheddar cheese, grated
pinch of cayenne pepper
2 tablespoons water
1 egg, beaten
poppy seeds, sunflower seeds or
sesame seeds, to decorate*

❧

1 Preheat the oven to 400°F. Grease two baking sheets. Sift the flour, dry mustard and salt into a bowl and rub in the butter until the mixture resembles fine bread crumbs.

2 Stir in the cheese and cayenne pepper and sprinkle on the water. Add half the beaten egg, mix to a firm dough and knead lightly until smooth.

3 Roll out the dough on a lightly floured surface and cut out a variety of shapes. Re-roll the trimmings and cut more shapes.

4 Place on the prepared baking sheets and brush with the remaining egg. Sprinkle on the seeds. Bake for 8–10 minutes, until golden.

Cheese Straws

Makes 50 straws and 8 rings

❧

INGREDIENTS

*1 cup all-purpose flour, plus extra
for dusting
1 teaspoon mustard powder
pinch of salt
¹/₂ cup butter
¹/₄ cup Cheddar cheese, grated
pinch of cayenne pepper
2 tablespoons water
1 egg, beaten
poppy seeds, sunflower seeds or
sesame seeds, to decorate*

❧

1 Make the cheese pastry in the same way as Festive Nibbles. Cut the cheese pastry into fingers about 4 inches long and ¹/₄ inch wide.

2 Roll out the trimmings, cut rounds using two pastry cutters of different sizes, a 2¹/₂ inch one to cut out the circle and a 2 inch diameter one to stamp out the center. Cook as above.

3 To serve, push six or eight straws through each ring.

Savory Cheese Whirls

These make a tasty after-school treat for children.

Makes 16

❦

INGREDIENTS

*9 ounces frozen puff pastry,
defrosted
¹/₂ teaspoon vegetable
extract (Marmite)
1 egg, beaten
¹/₂ cup grated red Leicester or
Cheddar cheese
carrot and cucumber sticks, to
serve*

❦

1 Preheat the oven to 425°F. Grease a large baking sheet. Roll out the pastry on a floured surface to a large rectangle, about 14 x 10 inch.

2 Spread the pastry with vegetable extract, leaving a ¹/₂-inch border. Brush the edges of the pastry with egg and sprinkle over the cheese to cover the vegetable extract.

3 Roll the pastry up quite tightly like a jelly roll, starting from a longer edge. Brush the outside of the pastry with beaten egg.

4 Cut the pastry roll into thick slices and place on the prepared baking sheet.

5 Bake for 12–15 minutes, until the pastry is well risen and golden. Arrange on a serving plate and serve warm or cold with carrot and cucumber sticks.

Cook's Tip If the shapes become a little squashed when sliced, re-form into rounds by opening out the layers with the end of a knife.

Variation Omit the vegetable extract and use peanut butter, if preferred.

Cream Cheese Spirals

Makes 32

❦

INGREDIENTS

1 cup butter
1 cup cream cheese
2 teaspoons granulated sugar,
plus extra for sprinkling
2 cups all-purpose flour
1 egg white beaten with
1 tablespoon water, for glazing
For the filling
1 cup walnuts or pecans, finely
chopped
¹/₂ cup light brown sugar
1 teaspoon ground cinnamon

❦

1 With an electric mixer, cream the butter, cream cheese and sugar until soft. Sift over the flour and mix to form a dough. Gather into a ball and divide into halves. Flatten each piece, wrap in waxed paper and chill for at least 30 minutes.

2 To make the filling, mix together the chopped walnuts or pecans, brown sugar and cinnamon.

3 Preheat the oven to 375°F. Grease two baking sheets.

4 Roll out each half of dough thinly into a circle about 11 inches in diameter. Trim the edges with a knife, using a dinner plate as a guide.

5 Brush the surface with the egg white glaze and sprinkle the dough evenly with half the filling.

6 Cut the dough into quarters and each quarter into four sections, to form 16 triangles.

7 Starting from the base of the triangles, roll up to form spirals.

8 Place on the prepared baking sheets and brush with the remaining glaze. Sprinkle with granulated sugar. Bake for 15–20 minutes until golden. Transfer to a wire rack.

Bacon Twists

Making bread is always fun, so try this savory version and add that extra twist to breakfast.
Serve with soft cheese with herbs.

Makes 12

❦

INGREDIENTS

4 cups all-purpose flour
1 envelope easy-blend active
dry yeast
pinch of salt
1²/₃ cups hand-hot water
12 lean bacon strips
1 egg, beaten

❦

Cook's Tip The same basic dough mix can be used to make rolls or a loaf of bread. Tap the base of the loaf – if it sounds hollow, it's cooked.

2 Turn the dough onto a lightly floured surface and knead for 5 minutes, until the dough is smooth and elastic.

4 Place each bacon strip on a chopping board and run the back of the knife down its length, to stretch it slightly. Wind a strip of bacon around each dough "sausage."

1 Mix the flour, yeast and salt in a bowl and stir them together. Add a little of the water and mix with a knife. Add the remaining water and use your hands to pull the mixture together, to make a sticky dough.

3 Divide the dough into 12 even-size pieces and roll each one into a sausage shape. Lightly oil a baking sheet.

5 Brush the "sausages" with beaten egg and arrange them on the prepared baking sheet. Set aside in a warm place for 30 minutes, until doubled in size. Preheat the oven to 400°F. Bake the "sausages" for 20–25 minutes, until cooked and browned.

Variations Make some meat-free versions of these twists for vegetarians by twisting the dough by hand and sprinkling with poppy or sesame seeds before baking.

Wisconsin Cheddar and Chive Biscuits

These soft biscuits are delicious warm, split and spread with butter;

serve with soup or a main dish.

Makes 20

❧

INGREDIENTS

1¼ cups all-purpose flour
2 teaspoons baking powder
½ teaspoon baking soda
pinch of salt
¼ teaspoon black pepper
5 tablespoons unsalted butter,
chopped
½ cup grated aged Cheddar cheese
2 tablespoons chopped fresh
chives
¾ cup buttermilk

❧

Variation For Cheddar and Bacon
Biscuits, substitute 3 tablespoons
crumbled cooked bacon for the chives.

1 Preheat the oven to 400°F. Grease
a baking sheet.

2 Sift the flour, baking powder,
baking soda, salt and pepper into
a large bowl. Rub the butter into the
dry ingredients until the mixture
resembles coarse bread crumbs. Add
the cheese and chives and stir to mix.

3 Make a well in the center of the
mixture. Add the buttermilk and
stir vigorously until the batter comes
away from the sides of the bowl.

4 Drop in 2 tablespoon mounds
spaced 2–3 inches apart on the
prepared baking sheet. Bake for
12–15 minutes, until golden brown.

Corn Oysters

Serve hot by themselves or as an accompaniment to meat or chicken dishes.

Makes about 8

❧

INGREDIENTS

1 cup grated fresh corn kernels
1 egg, separated
2 tablespoons all-purpose flour
pinch of salt
¼ teaspoon black pepper
2–4 tablespoons butter or
margarine
2–4 tablespoons vegetable oil

❧

1 Combine the corn, egg yolk and
flour in a bowl. Mix well. Add
the salt and pepper.

2 In a separate bowl, beat the egg
white until it forms stiff peaks.
Fold it carefully into the corn
mixture.

3 Heat 2 tablespoons butter or
margarine with 2 tablespoons oil
in a frying pan. When the fats are
very hot and almost smoking, drop
tablespoonfuls of the corn mixture
into the pan. Fry until crisp and
brown on the undersides.

4 Turn the "oysters" over and cook
for 1–2 minutes on the other side.
Drain on paper towels and keep hot.
Continue frying the "oysters," adding
more fat as necessary.

Cook's Tip Thawed frozen or canned
corn kernels can also be used. Drain
them well and chop.

Cornmeal Biscuits

Serve these biscuits hot, spread with butter.

Makes 12

INGREDIENTS

*1¼ cups all-purpose flour
2½ teaspoons baking powder
pinch of salt
½ cup cornmeal, plus extra for
sprinkling
⅓ cup vegetable shortening or
butter, chopped
¾ cup milk*

1 Preheat the oven to 450°F. Sprinkle an ungreased baking sheet lightly with cornmeal.

2 Sift the flour, baking powder and salt into a bowl. Stir in the cornmeal. Rub the shortening or butter into the dry ingredients until the mixture resembles coarse bread crumbs.

3 Make a well in the center and pour in the milk. Stir in quickly with a wooden spoon until the dough begins to pull away from the sides.

4 Turn the dough onto a lightly floured surface and knead lightly 8–10 times only. Roll out to a thickness of ½ inch. Cut into rounds with a floured 2-inch cookie cutter.

5 Arrange on the prepared baking sheet, about 1 inch apart. Sprinkle with cornmeal. Bake for 10–12 minutes, until golden brown.

Thyme and Mustard Biscuits

These aromatic biscuits are delicious served with herbed cheese with a salad course at dinner.

Makes 40

❦

INGREDIENTS

1½ *cups wholewheat all-purpose flour*
²/₃ *cup medium oatmeal*
2 tablespoons superfine sugar
2 teaspoons baking powder
2 tablespoons fresh thyme leaves
4 tablespoons butter, chopped
2 tablespoons vegetable shortening, chopped
3 tablespoons milk
2 teaspoons Dijon mustard
2 tablespoons sesame seeds
salt and black pepper

❦

1 Preheat the oven to 400°F. Grease two baking sheets. Put the flour, oats, sugar, baking powder, thyme leaves and seasoning into a bowl and mix. Add the fats to the bowl, then rub in.

2 Mix the milk and mustard together and stir into the flour mixture until you have a soft dough.

3 Knead lightly on a floured surface then roll out to a thickness of ¼ inch. Stamp out 2-inch rounds with a floured fluted cookie cutter and arrange, spaced slightly apart, on the prepared baking sheets.

4 Re-roll the trimmings and continue stamping out biscuits until all the dough is used. Prick the biscuits with a fork and sprinkle with sesame seeds. Cook for 10–12 minutes, until lightly browned.

5 Cool on the sheets, then pack into a small airtight container. Store in a cool place for up to 5 days.

Salted Peanut Cookies

The combinaton of salt and sweet flavors is delicious.

Makes 70

❧

INGREDIENTS

3 cups all-purpose flour
¹/₂ teaspoon baking soda
¹/₂ cup butter
¹/₂ cup margarine
1¹/₂ cups light brown sugar
2 eggs
2 teaspoons vanilla extract
2 cups salted peanuts

❧

1 Preheat the oven to 375°F. Lightly grease two baking sheets. Grease the bottom of a glass and dip it in sugar.

2 Sift together the flour and baking soda. Set aside.

3 With an electric mixer, cream the butter, margarine and sugar until light and fluffy. Beat in the eggs and vanilla extract. Fold in the flour mixture.

Variation To make Cashew Cookies, substitute an equal amount of salted cashews for the peanuts, and add as above. The flavor is subtle and interesting.

4 Stir the peanuts into the butter mixture until evenly combined.

5 Drop teaspoonfuls 2 inches apart on the prepared sheets. Flatten with the prepared glass.

6 Bake for about 10 minutes, until lightly colored. With a metal spatula, transfer to a wire rack to cool completely.

Cheddar Pennies

Serve these tasty snacks with pre-dinner drinks.

Makes 20

❧

INGREDIENTS

4 tablespoons butter
1 cup Cheddar cheese, grated
¹/₃ cup all-purpose flour
pinch of salt
pinch of cayenne pepper

❧

1 With an electric mixer, cream the butter until soft.

2 Stir in the cheese, flour, salt and cayenne. Gather to form a dough.

3 Transfer to a lightly floured surface. Shape into a cylinder about 1¹/₄ inches in diameter. Wrap in waxed paper and chill for 1-2 hours.

4 Preheat the oven to 350°F. Grease 1-2 baking sheets.

5 Cut the dough into ¹/₄ inch thick slices and place on the prepared baking sheets. Bake for about 15 minutes, until golden. Transfer to a wire rack to cool.

Blue Cheese and Chive Crisps

Makes 48

❧

INGREDIENTS

2 cups blue cheese, crumbled
$^1/_2$ cup unsalted butter
1 egg
1 egg yolk
2 teaspoons chopped fresh chives
black pepper
2 cups all-purpose flour, sifted

❧

Cook's Tip The cheese crisps will keep up to 10 days in an airtight container.

1 The day before serving, beat together the cheese and butter until well blended. Add the egg, egg yolk, chives and a little pepper and beat until just blended.

2 Add the flour in three batches, folding in well between each addition.

3 Divide the dough in half and shape each half into a log about 2 inches in diameter. Wrap in waxed paper and chill overnight. Preheat the oven to 375°F. Lightly grease two baking sheets.

4 Cut the dough logs across into slices about $^1/_8$ inch thick. Place on the prepared baking sheets. Bake for about 10 minutes, until just golden around the edges. Transfer to a wire rack to cool.

Cheese Muffins

Makes 9

❦

INGREDIENTS

4 tablespoons butter
1¹/₂ cups all-purpose flour
2 teaspoons baking powder
2 tablespoons sugar
pinch of salt
1 teaspoon paprika
2 eggs
¹/₂ cup milk
1 teaspoon dried thyme
2 ounces aged Cheddar cheese, cut
into ¹/₂-inch dice

❦

1 Preheat the oven to 375°F. Grease nine muffin tins, or use paper liners. Melt the butter in a small saucepan.

2 In a mixing bowl, sift together the flour, baking powder, sugar, salt and paprika.

3 In another bowl, combine the eggs, milk, melted butter and thyme and whisk to blend.

4 Add the milk mixture to the dry ingredients and stir until just moistened; do not mix until smooth.

5 Place a heaping spoonful of batter into the prepared pans. Drop a few pieces of cheese over each, then top with another spoonful of batter.

6 Bake for about 25 minutes, until puffed and golden. Allow to stand for 5 minutes before unmolding onto a wire rack. These muffins are best served warm or at room temperature.

Bacon Cornmeal Muffins

Serve these muffins fresh from the oven for a special breakfast.

Makes 14

❧

INGREDIENTS

8 bacon strips
4 tablespoons butter
4 tablespoons margarine
1 cup all-purpose flour
1 tablespoon baking powder
1 teaspoon sugar
pinch of salt
1½ cups cornmeal
1 cup milk
2 eggs

❧

1 Preheat the oven to 400°F. Grease 14 muffin pans, or use paper liners.

2 Fry the bacon until crisp. Drain on paper towels, then chop into small pieces. Set aside. Melt the butter and margarine in a saucepan over low heat and set aside.

3 Sift the flour, baking powder, sugar and salt into a large mixing bowl. Stir in the cornmeal, then make a well in the center. In another saucepan, heat the milk to lukewarm. In a small bowl, lightly beat the eggs, then add to the milk. Stir in the melted fats.

4 Pour the milk mixture into the center of the well and stir until smooth and well blended.

5 Fold in the bacon. Spoon the batter into the prepared pans, filling them halfway. Bake for about 20 minutes, until risen and lightly colored.

Savory Parmesan Puffs

Makes 6

INGREDIENTS

½ cup freshly grated Parmesan
cheese
1 cup all-purpose flour
pinch of salt
1 tablespoon butter or margarine
2 eggs
1 cup milk

1 Preheat the oven to 450°F. Grease
six individual baking tins.
Sprinkle each pan with 1 tablespoon
of the grated Parmesan. Alternatively,
you can use ramekins, in which case,
heat them on a baking sheet in the
oven, then grease and sprinkle with
Parmesan just before filling. Sift the
flour and salt into a small bowl. Set
aside. Melt the butter or margarine in
a small saucepan.

2 In a mixing bowl, beat together
the eggs, milk and melted butter
or margarine. Add the flour mixture
and stir until smoothly blended.

3 Divide the batter evenly among
the containers, filling each
one about half full. Bake for 15
minutes, then sprinkle the tops of the
puffs with the remaining grated
Parmesan cheese. Reduce the heat
to 350°F and continue baking for
20–25 minutes, until the puffs are
firm and golden brown.

4 Remove the puffs from the oven.
To unmold, run a thin knife
around the inside of each container
to loosen them. Gently ease out, then
transfer to a wire rack to cool.

Herb Popovers

Makes 12

INGREDIENTS

2 tablespoons butter
3 eggs
1 cup milk
¾ cup all-purpose flour
pinch of salt
1 small sprig each mixed fresh
herbs, such as chives, tarragon,
dill and parsley

1 Preheat the oven to 425°F. Grease 12 small ramekins or popover pans. Melt the butter in a small saucepan over low heat.

2 With an electric mixer, beat the eggs until blended. Beat in the milk and melted butter.

3 Sift together the flour and salt, then beat into the egg mixture to combine thoroughly.

4 Strip the herb leaves from the stems and chop finely. Stir 2 tablespoons into the batter.

5 Pour the batter into the dishes or pans so they are half full.

6 Bake for 25–30 minutes, until golden. Do not open the oven door during baking time or the popovers may fall. For drier popovers, pierce each one with a knife after 30 minutes baking time and bake for 5 minutes more. Serve hot.

Cheese Popovers

Makes 12

INGREDIENTS

1½ tablespoons butter
3 eggs
1 cup milk
¾ cup all-purpose flour
pinch of salt
¼ teaspoon paprika
6 tablespoons freshly grated
Parmesan cheese

1 Preheat the oven to 425°F. Grease 12 small ramekins or popover pans. Melt the butter in a small saucepan over low heat.

2 With an electric mixer, beat the eggs until blended. Beat in the milk and melted butter.

3 Sift together the flour, salt, and paprika, then beat into the egg mixture. Add the cheese and stir.

4 Fill the prepared dishes or pans so they are half full. Bake for 25–30 minutes, until golden. Do not open the oven door during baking or the popovers will fall. For drier popovers, pierce each one with a knife after 30 minutes baking time and bake for 5 minutes more. Serve hot.

Tiny Cheese Puffs

*These bite-sized portions of choux pastry are the ideal accompaniment
to a glass of wine before dinner.*

Makes 45

❧

INGREDIENTS

*1 cup all-purpose flour
pinch of salt
1 teaspoon dry mustard
pinch of cayenne pepper
1 cup water
¹/₂ cup butter, chopped
4 eggs
3 ounces Gruyère or Swiss cheese,
finely diced
1 tablespoon finely chopped
chives*

❧

Cook's Tip The puffs can be prepared
ahead and are suitable for freezing.
Reheat in a hot oven for 5 minutes,
until crisp, before serving.

1 Preheat the oven to 400°F. Lightly
grease two large baking sheets.
Sift together the flour, salt, dry
mustard and cayenne pepper.

2 In a medium-sized saucepan,
bring the water and butter to a
boil over medium-high heat. Remove
from the heat and add the flour
mixture all at once, beating with a
wooden spoon until the dough forms
a ball. Return to the heat and beat
constantly for 1–2 minutes to dry
out. Remove from the heat and cool
for 3–5 minutes.

3 Beat three of the eggs into the
dough, one at a time, beating well
after each addition. Beat the fourth egg
in a small bowl and add a teaspoon at
a time, beating until the dough is
smooth and shiny and falls slowly
when dropped from a spoon. (You may
not need all of the fourth egg; reserve
any remaining egg for glazing.) Stir in
the diced cheese and chives.

4 Using two teaspoons, drop
small mounds of dough 2 inches
apart onto the prepared baking
sheets. Beat the reserved egg with
1 tablespoon water and brush the
tops with the glaze.

5 Bake for 8 minutes, then reduce
the oven temperature to 350°F
and bake for 7–8 minutes more, until
puffed and golden. Transfer to a wire
rack to cool. Serve warm.

Variation For Ham and Cheese Puffs,
add ¹/₄ cup finely diced ham with the
cheese. For Cheese Herb Puffs, stir in 2
tablespoons chopped fresh herbs or
scallions with the cheese.

Cheese Biscuits

*These delicious biscuits make a good tea-time treat. They are best served
fresh and still slightly warm.*

Makes 12

❧

INGREDIENTS

2 cups all-purpose flour
2¹/₂ teaspoons baking powder
¹/₂ teaspoon dry mustard
¹/₂ teaspoon salt
4 tablespoons cold butter, chopped
³/₄ cup Cheddar cheese, grated
²/₃ cup milk
1 egg, beaten

❧

1 Preheat the oven to 450°F. Sift
the flour, baking powder, dry
mustard and salt into a mixing bowl.
Add the butter and rub into the flour
mixture until the mixture resembles
bread crumbs.

2 Stir in ¹/₂ cup of the cheese into
the butter and flour mixture.

3 Make a well in the center and
gently stir in the milk and egg
until smooth. Turn the dough onto a
lightly floured surface.

4 Roll out the dough and cut into
triangles or squares. Brush lightly
with milk and sprinkle with the
remaining cheese. Allow to rest for
15 minutes, then bake for 15 minutes,
until well risen.

Oatcakes

These are very simple to make and are an excellent addition to a cheese board.

Makes 24

❧

INGREDIENTS

2 cups rolled oats, plus extra for
sprinkling
³/₄ cup all-purpose flour
¹/₄ teaspoon baking soda
1 teaspoon salt
2 tablespoons vegetable shortening
2 tablespoons butter

❧

1 Preheat the oven to 425°F. Place
the oats, flour, baking soda and
salt in a large bowl. Melt the two fats
together in a small saucepan over
low heat.

2 Add the melted fat and enough
boiling water to make a dough.
Turn onto a surface sprinkled with a
little oatmeal. Roll out thinly and cut
into 24 circles. Bake on ungreased
baking sheets for 15 minutes.

Ham and Sun-Dried Tomato Biscuits

These make an ideal accompaniment for soup. Choose a strongly flavored ham and chop it fairly finely, so that a little goes a long way.

Makes 12

INGREDIENTS

2 cups self-rising flour
1 teaspoon dry mustard
1 teaspoon paprika, plus extra
for sprinkling
pinch of salt
2 tablespoons margarine, chopped
1 tablespoon snipped fresh basil
1/3 cup drained sun-dried tomatoes
in oil, chopped
2 ounces Black Forest or Virginia
ham, chopped
1/4–1/2 cup skim milk, plus extra
for brushing

1 Preheat the oven to 400°F. Flour a large baking sheet. Sift the flour, mustard, paprika and salt into a bowl. Using your fingers, rub in the margarine until the mixture resembles bread crumbs.

2 Stir the basil, sun-dried tomatoes and ham into the bowl. Pour in enough milk to make a soft dough.

3 Turn the dough onto a lightly floured surface, knead lightly and roll out to an 8 x 6-inch rectangle. Cut into 2-inch squares and arrange on the baking sheet.

4 Brush the tops with milk, sprinkle with paprika and bake for 12–15 minutes. Transfer to a rack to cool.

Feta Cheese and Chive Biscuits

Feta cheese makes an excellent substitute for butter in these tangy savory biscuits.

Makes 9

Ⓥ

INGREDIENTS

1 cup self-rising white flour
1 cup self-rising whole wheat flour
pinch of salt
3 ounces feta cheese
1 tablespoon chopped fresh chives
²/₃ cup skim milk, plus extra for glazing
¹/₄ teaspoon cayenne pepper

Ⓥ

1 Preheat the oven to 400°F. Sift the flours and salt into a mixing bowl, adding any bran left over from the flour in the sieve.

2 Crumble the feta cheese and rub into the dry ingredients. Stir in the chives, then add the milk and mix to a soft dough.

3 Turn onto a floured surface and lightly knead until smooth. Roll out to ¹/₄-inch thick and stamp out nine biscuits with a floured 2¹/₂-inch cookie cutter.

4 Transfer to a nonstick baking sheet. Brush with skim milk, then sprinkle over the cayenne pepper. Bake for 15 minutes, until golden brown. Serve warm or cold.

Whole Wheat Herb Triangles

Stuffed with cooked chicken and salad, these make a good lunchtime snack, and are also an ideal accompaniment to a bowl of steaming soup.

Makes 8

❦

INGREDIENTS

2 cups whole wheat flour
1 cup all-purpose flour
pinch of salt
$\frac{1}{2}$ teaspoon baking soda
1 teaspoon cream of tartar
$\frac{1}{2}$ teaspoon cayenne pepper
$\frac{1}{4}$ cup margarine, chopped
4 tablespoons chopped mixed
fresh herbs
1 cup skim milk
1 tablespoon sesame seeds

❦

1 Preheat the oven to 425°F. Lightly flour a baking sheet. Put the whole wheat flour and all-purpose flour in a mixing bowl. Sift in the salt, baking soda, cream of tartar and cayenne pepper, then rub in the margarine.

2 Add the herbs and milk and mix quickly to a soft dough. Turn onto a lightly floured surface. Knead only very briefly or the dough will become tough.

3 Roll the dough out to a 9-inch round and place on the prepared baking sheet. Brush lightly with water and sprinkle the top evenly with the sesame seeds.

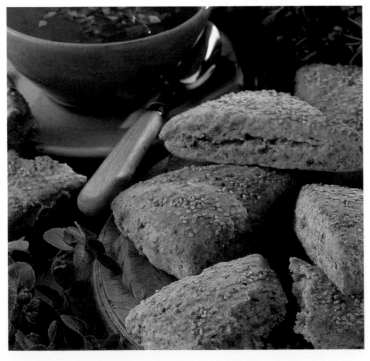

4 Carefully cut the dough round into eight wedges, separate them slightly and bake for 15–20 minutes. Transfer to a wire rack to cool. Serve warm or cold.

Variation To make Sun-Dried Tomato Triangles, replace the fresh mixed herbs with 2 tablespoons drained chopped sun-dried tomatoes in oil, and add 1 tablespoon each mild paprika, chopped fresh parsley and chopped fresh marjoram.

Dill and Potato Cakes

Makes 10

🌿

INGREDIENTS

2 cups self-rising flour
3 tablespoons butter
pinch of salt
1 tablespoon finely chopped fresh
dill
scant 1 cup mashed potato,
freshly made
2–3 tablespoons milk

🌿

1 Preheat the oven to 450°F. Sift the flour into a bowl, and add the butter, salt and dill. Mix in the potato and enough milk to make a soft dough.

2 Roll out the dough until fairly thin. Cut into neat rounds with a floured 3-inch cutter. Place the cakes on a greased baking sheet, and bake for 20–25 minutes.

Chive and Potato Biscuits

These biscuits should be fairly thin, soft and crisp on the outside. Serve them for breakfast.

Makes 20

❦

INGREDIENTS

1 pound potatoes
1 cup all-purpose flour
2 tablespoons olive oil
2 tablespoons chopped chives
salt and black pepper

❦

Cook's Tip Cook the biscuits over a constant low heat so the outsides do not burn before the insides are cooked through.

1 Cook the potatoes in a saucepan of boiling salted water for 20 minutes, until tender, then drain thoroughly. Return the potatoes to the clean pan and mash them. Preheat a griddle or heavy frying pan.

2 Add the flour, olive oil, chives and a little salt and pepper to the mashed potato. Mix to a soft dough.

3 Roll out the dough on a well-floured surface to a thickness of ¼ inch and stamp out rounds with a floured 2-inch plain biscuit cutter. Lightly grease the griddle or frying pan.

4 Cook the biscuits for about 10 minutes, turning once.

Curried Crackers

These spicy, crisp little crackers are ideal for serving with drinks.

Makes 12

ℳ

INGREDIENTS

¹/₂ cup all-purpose flour
pinch of salt
1 teaspoon curry powder
¹/₄ teaspoon cayenne pepper
1 tablespoon chopped cilantro
2 tablespoons water

ℳ

1 Preheat the oven to 350°F. Sift the flour and salt into a mixing bowl, then add the curry powder and cayenne pepper. Make a well in the center and add the chopped cilantro and water. Gradually incorporate the flour and mix to a firm dough.

2 Turn the dough onto a lightly floured surface, knead until smooth, then allow to rest for 5 minutes.

3 Cut the dough into 12 even-size pieces and knead into small balls. Roll each ball out very thinly to a 4-inch round, sprinkling more flour over the dough if necessary to prevent it from sticking to the rolling pin.

4 Arrange the rounds on two ungreased baking sheets, then bake for 15 minutes, turning over once during cooking. Transfer to a wire rack to cool.

Cocktail Shapes

These are made to order for a bridge party, or any party, using different flavors and shapes.

Makes 80

❧

INGREDIENTS

3 cups all-purpose flour
pinch of salt
$^1/_2$ teaspoon black pepper
1 teaspoon whole-grain mustard
$^3/_4$ cup butter, chopped
4 ounces Cheddar cheese
1 egg, beaten
1 teaspoon chopped nuts
2 teaspoons dill seeds
2 teaspoons curry paste
2 teaspoons chili sauce

❧

1 Preheat the oven to 400°F. Line several baking sheets with baking parchment. Sift the flour into a mixing bowl and add the salt, pepper and mustard.

2 Rub the butter into the flour mixture until it resembles fine bread crumbs. Grate the cheese, then with a fork stir it into the butter and flour mixture. Add the egg and mix together to form a soft dough.

3 Knead lightly on a floured surface and cut into four equal pieces.

4 Knead chopped nuts into one piece, dill seeds into another piece and curry paste and chili sauce into each of the remaining pieces. Wrap each piece of flavored dough in plastic wrap and chill for at least 1 hour. Remove from the plastic wrap and roll out one piece at a time.

5 Using a floured heart-shaped cutter, stamp out about 20 shapes from the curry-flavored dough and use a club-shaped cutter to cut out the chili-flavored dough. Arrange the shapes well spaced apart on the prepared baking sheets and bake in the oven for 6–8 minutes, until slightly puffed and pale gold in color. Cool on wire racks.

6 Repeat with the remaining flavored dough using spade- and diamond-shaped cutters. Knead any trimmings together, re-roll and stamp out and bake as above.

Spiced Cocktail Biscuits

These savory biscuits go perfectly with pre-dinner drinks.

Each of the spice seeds contributes to the flavor.

Makes 20–30

❦

INGREDIENTS

1¼ cups all-purpose flour
2 teaspoons curry powder
½ cup butter, chopped
¼ cup grated Cheddar cheese,
2 teaspoons poppy seeds
1 teaspoon nigella seeds
1 egg yolk
cumin seeds, to garnish

❦

Variation Use caraway or sesame seeds instead of the poppy seeds if you wish.

1 Grease two baking sheets. Sift the flour and curry powder into a large bowl. Rub in the butter until the mixture resembles bread crumbs, then stir in the cheese, poppy seeds and nigella seeds. Stir in the egg yolk and mix to a firm dough. Wrap the dough in plastic wrap and chill for 30 minutes.

3 Preheat the oven to 375°F. Bake for approximately 20 minutes, until crisp and golden. Serve warm or cold.

2 Roll out the dough on a floured surface to a thickness of about ⅛ inch. Cut into rounds with a floured cookie cutter. Arrange on the prepared baking sheets and sprinkle with the cumin seeds. Chill for 15 minutes.

Brownies
and Bars

A brownie should be a moist, chewy bar, crisp on the outside but slightly underdone inside. There are many recipes for brownies, varying in richness.

Bars are the quickest and easiest cookies to shape evenly. The cookie mixture is simply poured or pressed into the pan, baked, then cut to the required size with a large, sharp knife while still warm from the oven.

Some bar cookies are just a single layer, while others are double- or even triple-layered. The layers are sometimes added before baking, sometimes part way through the cooking, depending on the recipe.

Try to use the size pan stated in a recipe. If you use one that is smaller, the layer of mixture will be deeper so the outside of the bars will become overcooked and too brown and crisp or hard before the inside is ready, whereas if too large a pan is used the mixture will be spread too thinly, and not only will it cook too quickly and dry out, but the contrast of moist center to crisp crust will be lessened. If you only have a larger pan, the size can be reduced by making a wide strip formed from a triple thickness of foil to fit across the pan at the right place. Fold up along a long edge to make a lap that the weight of the mixture will hold down, keeping the foil divider in place.

Bar cookies can be stored for a day or so in their baking pan. Cover the pan as tightly as you can with foil, or slide it into a plastic bag, gently press out as much air as possible and seal tightly.

White Chocolate Brownies

Makes 16

INGREDIENTS

1¼ cups all-purpose flour
½ teaspoon baking powder
pinch of salt
6 ounces good-quality white
chocolate, chopped
½ cup sugar
½ cup unsalted butter, chopped
2 eggs, lightly beaten
1 teaspoon vanilla extract
6 ounces semisweet chocolate,
chopped; or chocolate chips
For the topping
7 ounces milk chocolate, chopped
2 cups unsalted macadamia nuts,
chopped

1 Preheat the oven to 350°F. Grease a 9-inch springform pan. Sift together the flour, baking powder and salt. Set aside.

2 In a medium saucepan over medium heat, melt the white chocolate, sugar and butter, stirring until smooth.

3 Cool slightly, then beat in the eggs and vanilla extract. Stir in the flour until well blended. Stir in the chopped chocolate or chocolate chips. Spread evenly in the prepared pan, smoothing the top.

4 Bake for 20–25 minutes, until a skewer inserted 2 inches from the side of the pan comes out clean. Remove from the oven. Sprinkle chopped milk chocolate evenly over the surface (avoid touching the side of the pan) and return to the oven for 1 minute.

5 Remove from the oven and, using the back of a spoon, spread the softened chocolate evenly over the top. Sprinkle with the macadamia nuts and gently press into the chocolate. Cool on a wire rack for 30 minutes, then chill until set. Run a sharp knife around the side of the pan to loosen; unclip the pan side and carefully remove. Cut into thin wedges.

Marbled Brownies

Makes 24

❦

INGREDIENTS

8 ounces semisweet chocolate,
chopped
⅓ cup butter, chopped
4 eggs
1½ cups sugar
1 cup all-purpose flour
pinch of salt
1 teaspoon baking powder
2 teaspoons vanilla extract
1 cup walnuts, chopped
For the plain batter
4 tablespoons butter
⅔ cup cream cheese
½ cup sugar
2 eggs
2 tablespoons all-purpose flour
1 teaspoon vanilla extract

❦

1 Preheat the oven to 350°F. Line a 13 x 9-inch pan with waxed paper and grease the paper.

2 Melt the chocolate and butter in a saucepan over very low heat.

3 Meanwhile, beat the eggs until light and fluffy. Gradually add the sugar and continue beating until blended. Sift over the flour, salt and baking powder and fold in.

4 Stir in the cooled chocolate mixture and the vanilla extract and walnuts. Set aside 2 cups of the chocolate batter.

5 To make the plain batter, cream the butter and cream cheese with an electric mixer.

6 Add the sugar and continue beating until blended. Beat in the eggs, flour and vanilla extract.

7 Spread the unmeasured chocolate batter into the pan. Pour over the cream cheese mixture. Drop spoonfuls of the reserved chocolate batter on top.

8 With a metal spatula, swirl the mixtures to marble. Do not blend completely. Bake for 35–40 minutes, until just set. Unmold when cool and cut into squares for serving.

Fudge-Glazed Chocolate Slices

Makes 8–10

❦

INGREDIENTS

11 ounces semisweet chocolate,
chopped
¹/₂ cup unsalted butter, chopped
generous ¹/₂ cup firmly packed
light brown sugar
¹/₄ cup granulated sugar
2 eggs
1 tablespoon vanilla extract
¹/₂ cup all-purpose flour
1 cup pecans or walnuts, toasted
and chopped
5 ounces good-quality white
chocolate, chopped
For the Fudge Glaze
6 ounces semisweet chocolate,
chopped
4 tablespoons unsalted butter,
chopped
2 tablespoons light corn syrup
2 teaspoons vanilla extract
1 teaspoon instant coffee powder
pecan halves, to decorate
(optional)

❦

1 Preheat the oven to 350°F. Invert
an 8-inch square baking pan and
mold a piece of foil over the bottom.
Turn the pan over and line with
molded foil. Lightly grease the foil.

2 In a medium saucepan over low
heat, melt the semisweet chocolate
and butter, stirring until smooth.

3 Stir in the sugars and continue
stirring for 2 minutes, until the
sugar has dissolved. Beat in the eggs
and vanilla extract. Stir in the flour,
nuts and white chocolate. Pour the
batter into the prepared pan.

4 Bake for 20–25 minutes, until a
skewer inserted 2 inches from
the center comes out clean. Remove
the pan to a wire rack to cool for
30 minutes. Using the foil, lift from
the pan and cool on the wire rack
for 2 hours.

5 To make the glaze, melt the
chocolate, butter, syrup, vanilla
extract and coffee powder in a
medium saucepan over medium heat,
stirring frequently, until smooth.
Remove from the heat. Chill for
1 hour, until thickened and
spreadable.

6 Invert the cake onto the wire
rack, and remove the foil from
the bottom. Turn top side up. Using
a metal spatula, spread a thick layer
of fudge glaze over the top of the
cake just to the edges. Chill for
1 hour, until set. Cut into squares or
fingers. If you wish, top each with a
pecan half.

Chocolate Brownies

Wonderful old-fashioned brownies are usually high in fat. This no-butter version still tastes rich and mellow but is best eaten on the day it is made.

Makes 20

INGREDIENTS

½ cup sunflower oil
5 ounces semisweet chocolate,
chopped
2 eggs
1 cup self-rising flour
½ cup sugar
1 teaspoon vanilla extract
¾ cup halved pecans

1 Preheat the oven to 400°F. Use a little of the oil to grease a 9-inch square shallow cake pan and line with lightly oiled waxed paper.

Cook's Tip Ingredients can be melted easily in the microwave. To soften chocolate, butter, sugar or syrup, microwave on full power for a few minutes, until soft.

2 Melt the chocolate with the remaining oil in a heatproof bowl over a saucepan of water, stirring until smooth.

3 Beat the eggs lightly and add them to the chocolate, stirring vigorously. Beat in the flour, sugar and vanilla extract and pour the mixture into the prepared pan. Arrange the pecans over the top.

4 Bake for 10–15 minutes. If you like chewy brownies, take them out of the oven now. If you want a more cake-like finish, leave for another 5 minutes. Cut into squares and allow to cool before removing from the pan.

Nut and Chocolate Chip Brownies

These brownies are moist, dark and deeply satisfying.

Makes 16

❦

INGREDIENTS

5 ounces semisweet chocolate,
chopped
$\frac{1}{2}$ cup sunflower oil
$1\frac{1}{4}$ cups firmly packed light
brown sugar
2 eggs
1 teaspoon vanilla extract
$\frac{2}{3}$ cup self-rising flour
4 tablespoons cocoa powder
$\frac{3}{4}$ cup chopped walnuts or pecans
4 tablespoons milk chocolate
chips

❦

Cook's Tip These brownies will freeze
for 3 months in an airtight container.

1 Preheat the oven to 350°F. Lightly
grease a shallow 7½-inch square
cake pan. Melt the semisweet
chocolate in a heatproof bowl over a
saucepan of hot water.

2 With an electric mixer, beat the
oil, sugar, eggs and vanilla
extract together in a large bowl.

3 Stir in the melted chocolate, then
beat well until evenly mixed.

4 Sift the flour and cocoa powder
into the bowl and fold in
thoroughly. Stir in the chopped nuts
and chocolate chips, pour into the
prepared pan and spread evenly to the
edges. Bake for 30–35 minutes, until
the top is firm and crusty. Cool in the
pan before cutting into squares.

Banana Gingerbread

This gingerbread keeps well and actually improves with age. Store it in a covered container for up to 2 months.

Makes 26

❧

INGREDIENTS

1¾ cups all-purpose flour
2 teaspoons baking soda
2 teaspoons ground ginger
1¼ cups rolled oats
4 tablespoons dark brown sugar
⅓ cup margarine, chopped
⅔ cup light corn syrup
1 egg, beaten
3 ripe bananas, mashed
¾ cup confectioners' sugar
crystallized ginger, to decorate

❧

Cook's Tip These nutritious, energy-giving squares are a really good choice for packed lunches, as they don't break up too easily.

1 Preheat the oven to 325°F. Grease and line a 7 x 11-inch cake pan.

2 Sift together the flour, baking soda and ground ginger, then stir in the oats. Melt the sugar, margarine and syrup in a saucepan over low heat, then stir into the flour mixture. Beat in the egg and mashed bananas.

3 Spoon into the prepared pan and bake for about 1 hour, until firm to the touch. Allow to cool in the pan, then turn out and cut into squares.

4 Sift the confectioners' sugar into a bowl and stir in just enough water to make a smooth, runny icing. Drizzle the icing over each square and top with a piece of crystallized ginger.

Gingerbread Squares

The flavor of these squares will improve if they are stored in an airtight container for several days before serving.

Makes 16–20

❦

INGREDIENTS

1¼ cups milk
¾ cup light corn syrup
¾ cup molasses
½ cup butter or margarine, chopped
⅓ cup dark brown sugar
4 cups all-purpose flour
½ teaspoon baking soda
1¼ teaspoons ground ginger
4 cups rolled oats
1 egg, beaten
confectioners' sugar for dusting

❦

1 Preheat the oven to 350°F. Grease and line the base of a 8-inch square cake pan. Gently heat together the milk, syrup, molasses, butter or margarine and sugar, stirring until smooth; do not boil.

2 Stir together the flour, baking soda, ginger and oats. Make a well in the center, pour in the egg, then slowly pour in the warmed mixture, stirring to make a smooth batter.

3 Pour the batter into the pan and bake for about 45 minutes, until firm to the touch. Cool slightly in the pan, then cool completely on a wire rack. Cut into squares and dust with confectioners' sugar.

Chocolate Pecan Squares

Makes 16

INGREDIENTS

2 eggs
2 teaspoons vanilla extract
pinch of salt
1¹/₂ cups pecans, coarsely chopped
¹/₂ cup all-purpose flour
4 tablespoons sugar
¹/₂ cup molasses
3 ounces semisweet chocolate,
  finely chopped
3 tablespoons butter
16 pecan halves for decorating

1 Preheat the oven to 325°F. Line the bottom and sides of an 8-inch square baking pan with waxed paper and grease lightly.

2 Beat together the eggs, vanilla extract and salt. In another bowl, mix together the pecans and flour. Set both bowls aside.

3 In a saucepan, bring the sugar and molasses to a boil.

4 Remove from the heat and stir in the chocolate and butter and blend thoroughly with a wooden spoon.

5 Mix in the beaten eggs, then fold in the pecan mixture. Pour the batter into the prepared pan and bake for about 35 minutes, until set.

6 Cool in the pan for 10 minutes before unmolding. Cut into 2 inches squares and press pecan halves into the tops while warm. Cool completely on a wire rack.

Raisin Brownies

Makes 16

INGREDIENTS

¹/₂ cup butter or margarine,
  chopped
¹/₂ cup cocoa powder
2 eggs
1 cup sugar
1 teaspoon vanilla extract
¹/₃ cup all-purpose flour
³/₄ cup walnuts, chopped
¹/₂ cup raisins

1 Preheat the oven to 350°F. Line an 8-inch square baking pan with waxed paper and grease the paper.

2 Melt the butter or margarine in a small saucepan over low heat. Remove from the heat and stir in the cocoa powder.

3 With an electric mixer, beat together the eggs, sugar, and vanilla extract until light. Add the cocoa mixture and stir to blend.

4 Sift the flour over the cocoa mixture and gently fold in. Add the walnuts and raisins and scrape the batter into the prepared pan. Bake for 30 minutes. Do not overbake.

5 Leave in the pan to cool before cutting into 2-inch squares and removing. The brownies should be soft and moist. Dust with confectioners' sugar before serving.

Chocolate Butterscotch Bars

Makes 24

❧

INGREDIENTS

2 cups all-purpose flour
$^{1}/_{2}$ teaspoon baking powder
$^{1}/_{2}$ cup unsalted butter, chopped
$^{1}/_{3}$ cup light brown sugar
5 ounces semisweet chocolate, melted
2 tablespoons ground almonds
For the topping
$^{3}/_{4}$ cup unsalted butter
$^{1}/_{2}$ cup granulated sugar
2 tablespoons light corn syrup
$^{3}/_{4}$ cup condensed milk
1$^{1}/_{4}$ cups whole toasted hazelnuts
8 ounces semisweet chocolate, chopped

❧

1 Preheat the oven to 325°F. Grease a shallow 12 x 8-inch cake pan. Sift the flour and baking powder into a large bowl. Rub in the butter, then stir in the sugar. Work in the melted chocolate and ground almonds.

2 Press the mixture into the prepared cake pan, prick the surface with a fork and bake for 25–30 minutes, until firm. Allow to cool.

3 To make the topping, mix the butter, sugar, light corn syrup and condensed milk in a saucepan. Heat gently until the butter and sugar have melted. Simmer, stirring occasionally, until golden, then stir in the hazelnuts.

4 Pour over the cooked base and spread out evenly. Allow to set.

5 Melt the chocolate in a bowl over a saucepan of hot water. Spread over the butterscotch layer; allow to set before cutting into bars.

Brownies and Bars

Sour Cream Streusel Bars

A deliciously different tea-time treat.

Makes 12–14

❧

INGREDIENTS

$^1/_2$ cup butter
$^2/_3$ cup granulated sugar
3 eggs, at room temperature
$1^1/_2$ cups all-purpose flour
1 teaspoon baking soda
1 teaspoon baking powder
1 cup sour cream
For the topping
1 firmly packed cup dark brown
sugar
2 teaspoons ground cinnamon
1 cup walnuts, finely chopped
4 tablespoons butter, chopped

❧

1 Preheat the oven to 350°F. Line the bottom of a 9-inch square cake pan with waxed paper and grease the paper.

4 Add the eggs, one at a time, beating well after each addition.

5 In another bowl, sift the flour, baking soda and baking powder together three times.

7 Pour half of the batter into the prepared pan and sprinkle over half of the topping.

8 Pour the remaining batter on top and sprinkle over the remaining topping.

2 To make the topping, place the brown sugar, cinnamon and walnuts in a bowl. Mix with your fingertips, then add the butter and continue working until the mixture resembles coarse crumbs.

3 Cream the butter with an electric mixer until soft. Add the sugar and continue beating until the mixture is light and fluffy.

6 Fold the dry ingredients into the butter mixture in three batches, alternating with the sour cream. Fold until blended after each addition.

9 Bake for 60–70 minutes, until browned. Allow to stand for 5 minutes, then unmold and transfer to a wire rack to cool.

163

White Chocolate Macadamia Slices

*Keep these treats for someone special who will really appreciate
their superb rich flavor and crunchy texture.*

Makes 16

❦

INGREDIENTS

*1¼ cups macadamia nuts,
blanched almonds or hazelnuts
14 ounces white chocolate,
chopped
⅓ cup dried apricots
⅓ cup unsalted butter
1 teaspoon vanilla extract
3 eggs
scant 1 cup firmly packed light
brown sugar
1 cup self-rising flour*

❦

1 Preheat the oven to 375°F. Lightly
grease two 8-inch cake pans and
line the bottom of each with waxed
paper or baking parchment.

2 Coarsely chop the nuts and half
the white chocolate, making sure
that the pieces are more or less the
same size, then cut up the apricots to
similar-size pieces.

3 In the top of a double boiler or in
a heatproof bowl over a saucepan
of hot water, melt the remaining
white chocolate over gentle heat
with the butter, stirring occasionally
until smooth. Remove the bowl from
the heat.

4 Stir in the vanilla extract. Beat
the eggs and sugar in a mixing
bowl until thick and pale, then beat
in the melted chocolate mixture.

6 Spoon the mixture into the
prepared pans, smooth the top
level and bake for 30–35 minutes.

Cook's Tip It is easier to cut these
bars after they have cooled. Use a
serrated knife.

5 Sift the flour over the mixture
and fold it in evenly. Stir in the
nuts, white chocolate and apricots.

Toffee Bars

Makes 32

❦

INGREDIENTS

2 cups firmly packed light
brown sugar
2 cups butter or margarine
2 egg yolks
1¹/₂ teaspoons vanilla extract
4 cups all-purpose or
whole wheat flour
pinch of salt
8 ounces milk chocolate, chopped
1 cup walnuts or pecans, chopped

❦

1 Preheat the oven to 350°F. Grease a 13 x 9 x 2-inch cake pan. Beat together the sugar and butter or margarine until light and fluffy. Beat in the egg yolks and vanilla extract. Stir in the flour and salt.

2 Spread the dough in the prepared cake pan. Bake for 25–30 minutes, until lightly browned. The texture will be soft.

3 Remove from the oven and immediately place the chocolate pieces on the hot cookie base. Let it stand until the chocolate softens, then spread it evenly with a spatula. Sprinkle with the nuts. While still warm, cut into about 2 x 1¹/₂-inch bars.

Variation Use chopped pecan nuts instead of walnuts if you prefer, or try a mixture of both.

Chocolate Walnut Bars

Makes 24

INGREDIENTS

½ cup walnuts
⅓ cup granulated sugar
¾ cup all-purpose flour, sifted
6 tablespoons cold unsalted
butter, chopped
For the topping
2 tablespoons unsalted butter
⅓ cup water
⅓ cup cocoa powder
½ cup granulated sugar
1 teaspoon vanilla extract
pinch of salt
2 eggs
confectioners' sugar for dusting

1 Preheat the oven to 350°F. Grease the sides and bottom of an 8-inch square cake pan.

2 Grind the walnuts with a few tablespoons of the sugar in a food processor, blender or nut grinder.

3 In a bowl, combine the ground walnuts, the remaining sugar, and the flour. Rub in the butter until the mixture resembles coarse crumbs. Alternatively, put all the ingredients in a food processor and process until the mixture resembles coarse crumbs.

4 Pat the walnut mixture into the bottom of the prepared pan in an even layer. Bake for 25 minutes.

5 Meanwhile, to make the topping, melt the butter with the water in a small saucepan over low heat. Beat in the cocoa and sugar.

6 Remove the pan from the heat, stir in the vanilla extract and salt and allow to cool for 5 minutes.

7 Beat in the eggs until blended. Pour the topping evenly over the crust when it is cooked.

8 Return to the oven and bake for about 20 minutes, until set. Place the pan on a wire rack to cool. Cut into 2½ x 1-inch bars and dust with confectioners' sugar. Store in the refrigerator.

Pecan Squares

Makes 36

❦

INGREDIENTS

2 cups all-purpose flour
pinch of salt
$^{1}/_{2}$ cup granulated sugar
1 cup cold butter or margarine,
chopped
1 egg
finely grated rind of 1 lemon
For the topping
$^{3}/_{4}$ cup butter
$^{1}/_{4}$ cup honey
$^{1}/_{4}$ cup granulated sugar
$^{1}/_{2}$ cup firmly packed dark
brown sugar
5 tablespoons whipping cream
4 cups pecan halves

❦

1 Preheat the oven to 375°F. Lightly grease a 15$^{1}/_{2}$ x 10$^{1}/_{2}$ x 1-inch jelly roll pan.

2 Sift the flour and salt into a mixing bowl. Stir in the sugar. Cut and rub in the butter or margarine until the mixture resembles coarse crumbs. Add the egg and lemon rind and blend with a fork until the mixture just holds together.

3 Spoon the mixture into the prepared pan. With floured fingertips, press into an even layer. Prick the pastry all over with a fork and chill for 10 minutes.

4 Bake the pastry crust for 15 minutes. Remove the pan from the oven, but keep the oven on while making the topping.

5 To make the topping, melt the butter, honey and both sugars. Bring to a boil. Boil, without stirring, for 2 minutes. Remove from the heat and stir in the cream and pecans. Pour over the crust, return to the oven and bake for 25 minutes. Cool.

6 When cool, run a knife around the edge. Invert onto a baking sheet, place another sheet on top and invert again. Dip a sharp knife into very hot water and cut into squares for serving.

Hazelnut Squares

Makes 9

❦

INGREDIENTS

*2 ounces semisweet chocolate,
chopped*
¹/₃ cup butter or margarine
1 cup sugar
¹/₂ cup all-purpose flour
¹/₂ teaspoon baking powder
2 eggs, beaten
¹/₂ teaspoon vanilla extract
*1 cup skinned hazelnuts,
coarsely chopped*

❦

1 Preheat the oven to 350°F. Grease a 8-inch square cake pan.

2 In a heatproof bowl set over a saucepan of hot water, melt the chocolate and butter or margarine, stirring until smooth.

3 Add the sugar, flour, baking powder, eggs, vanilla extract and half of the hazelnuts to the mixture and stir with a wooden spoon.

4 Pour the mixture into the prepared cake pan. Bake for 10 minutes, then sprinkle the remaining hazelnuts over the top. Return to the oven and continue baking for about 25 minutes, until firm to the touch.

5 Allow to cool in the pan, set on a wire rack, for 10 minutes, then transfer to the rack and allow to cool completely. Cut into squares for serving.

Almond-Topped Squares

Makes 18

❦

INGREDIENTS

6 tablespoons butter
$^1/_4$ cup sugar
1 egg yolk
grated rind and juice of $^1/_2$ lemon
$^1/_2$ teaspoon vanilla extract
2 tablespoons whipping cream
1 cup all-purpose flour
For the topping
1 cup sugar
$^3/_4$ cup sliced almonds
4 egg whites
$^1/_2$ teaspoon ground ginger
$^1/_2$ teaspoon ground cinnamon

❦

1 Preheat the oven to 375°F. Line a 13 x 9-inch jelly roll pan with waxed paper and grease the paper.

2 With an electric mixer, cream the butter and sugar until light and fluffy. Beat in the egg yolk, lemon rind and juice, the vanilla extract and cream.

3 Gradually stir in the flour. Gather into a ball of dough. With lightly floured fingers, press the dough into the prepared pan. Bake for 15 minutes. Remove from the oven but leave the oven on.

4 To make the topping, combine all the ingredients in a heavy saucepan. Cook, stirring, until the mixture comes to a boil. Boil for 1 minute. Pour over the dough, spreading evenly.

5 Return to the oven and bake for about 45 minutes. Remove and score, then cut into bars or squares.

Lemon Squares

Makes 12

❧

INGREDIENTS

2 cups all-purpose flour
¹/₂ cup confectioners' sugar
pinch of salt
³/₄ cup butter or margarine
1 teaspoon cold water
For the lemon layer
4 eggs
2 cups granulated sugar
2 tablespoons all-purpose flour
¹/₂ teaspoon baking powder
1 teaspoon grated lemon rind
¹/₄ cup fresh lemon juice
confectioners' sugar for sprinkling

❧

1 Preheat the oven to 350°F. Sift the flour, confectioners' sugar and salt into a mixing bowl.

2 Rub the butter or margarine into the flour until the mixture resembles coarse bread crumbs. Add the water and toss lightly with a fork until the mixture forms a ball.

3 Press the mixture evenly into an ungreased 13 x 9-inch baking dish. Bake for 15–20 minutes, until light golden brown. Remove from the oven and allow to cool slightly.

4 Meanwhile, to make the lemon layer, beat together the eggs, granulated sugar, flour, baking powder and lemon rind and juice.

5 Pour the lemon mixture over the hot crust. Return to the oven and bake for 25 minutes. Allow to cool in the baking dish, placed on a wire rack.

6 Before serving, sprinkle the top with confectioners' sugar. Cut into squares with a sharp knife.

Apricot and Almond Fingers

These apricot and almond fingers will stay moist for several days.

Makes 18

❧

INGREDIENTS

2 cups self-rising flour
²/₃ cup firmly packed light
brown sugar
¹/₃ cup semolina
1 cup dried apricots, chopped
2 eggs
2 tablespoons malt extract
2 tablespoons honey
4 tablespoons skim milk
4 tablespoons sunflower oil
few drops of almond extract
2 tablespoons slivered almonds

❧

1 Preheat the oven to 325°F. Lightly grease and line an 11 x 7-inch shallow cake pan. Sift the flour into a bowl and add the brown sugar, semolina, dried apricots and eggs. Add the malt extract, honey, milk, sunflower oil and almond extract. Mix well until smooth.

2 Turn the mixture into the prepared cake pan, spread to the edges and sprinkle with the slivered almonds.

3 Bake for 30–35 minutes, until the center of the cake springs back when lightly pressed. Transfer to a wire rack to cool. Remove the paper, place the cake on a board and cut it into 18 slices with a sharp knife.

Apricot Bars

Makes 12

❦

INGREDIENTS

½ cup firmly packed light brown
sugar
¼ cup all-purpose flour
⅓ cup cold unsalted butter,
chopped
For the topping
1 cup dried apricots
1 cup water
grated rind of 1 lemon
⅓ cup granulated sugar
2 teaspoons cornstarch
½ cup walnuts, chopped

❦

1 Preheat the oven to 350°F. Grease
a 8-inch square cake pan.

2 In a bowl, combine the brown
sugar and flour. Rub in the butter
until the mixture resembles crumbs.

3 Press into the prepared cake pan.
Bake for 15 minutes. Remove
from the oven but leave the oven on.

4 To make the topping, combine the
apricots and water in a saucepan
and simmer for about 10 minutes,
until soft. Strain the liquid and
reserve. Chop the apricots.

5 Return the apricots to the
saucepan and add the lemon rind,
granulated sugar, cornstarch, and
4 tablespoons of the soaking liquid.
Cook for 1 minute.

6 Cool slightly before spreading the
topping over the base. Sprinkle
over the walnuts and continue baking
for 20 minutes more. Allow to cool in
the pan before cutting into bars.

Blueberry Streusel Slices

Makes 30

❧

INGREDIENTS

8 ounces pie-crust pastry
$\frac{1}{2}$ cup all-purpose flour
$\frac{1}{4}$ teaspoon baking powder
3 tablespoons butter or margarine
2 tablespoons fresh white
bread crumbs
$\frac{1}{3}$ cup light brown sugar
pinch of salt
4 tablespoons slivered or chopped
almonds
4 tablespoons blackberry or
other berry jam
scant 1 cup blueberries,
fresh or frozen

❧

1 Preheat the oven to 350°F. Roll out the pastry on a lightly floured surface to fit a 7 x 11-inch jelly roll pan. Grease the jelly roll pan.

2 Rub together the flour, baking powder, butter or margarine, bread crumbs, sugar and salt until really crumbly, then mix in the almonds.

3 Place the rolled pastry in the prepared pan. Spread the pastry with the jam, sprinkle with the blueberries, then cover evenly with the streusel topping, pressing down lightly. Bake for 30–40 minutes, lowering the temperature after 20 minutes to 325°F.

4 Remove from the oven. Cut into slices while still hot, then transfer to a wire rack to cool.

Sticky Date and Apple Squares

If possible, allow this mixture to mature for 1–2 days before cutting.

Makes 16

❧

INGREDIENTS

$\frac{1}{2}$ cup margarine
4 tablespoons dark brown sugar
4 tablespoons light corn syrup
$\frac{2}{3}$ cup chopped dates
$1\frac{1}{3}$ cups rolled oats
1 cup whole wheat self-rising
flour
2 eating apples, peeled,
cored and grated
1–2 teaspoons lemon juice
16 walnut halves

❧

1 Preheat the oven to 375°F. Line a 7 or 8-inch square or rectangle loose-bottomed cake pan. In a large saucepan, gently heat the margarine, sugar and syrup together until the margarine has melted completely.

2 Add the dates and cook until they have softened. Gradually work in the oats, flour, apples and lemon juice until well mixed.

3 Spoon into the prepared pan and spread out evenly. Top with the walnut halves. Bake for 30 minutes, then reduce the temperature to 325°F and bake for 10–12 minutes more, until firm to the touch and golden.

4 Cut into squares or bars while still warm if you are going to eat them right away, or wrap in foil when nearly cold and keep for 1–2 days before eating.

Spiced Fig Bars

Makes 48

❧

INGREDIENTS

*2 cups dried figs
3 eggs
³/₄ cup granulated sugar
³/₄ cup all-purpose flour
1 teaspoon baking powder
¹/₂ teaspoon ground cinnamon
¹/₄ teaspoon ground cloves
¹/₄ teaspoon grated nutmeg
pinch of salt
³/₄ cup walnuts, finely chopped
2 tablespoons brandy or cognac
confectioners' sugar for dusting*

❧

1 Preheat the oven to 325°F. Line a 12 x 8 x 1¹/₂-inch cake pan with waxed paper and grease the paper.

2 With a sharp knife, chop the figs coarsely. Set aside.

3 In a bowl, beat the eggs and sugar until well blended. In another bowl, sift together the dry ingredients, then fold into the egg mixture in several batches.

4 Stir the figs, walnuts and brandy or cognac into the bowl until evenly combined.

5 Scrape the mixture into the prepared cake pan and bake for 35–40 minutes, until the top is firm and brown. It should still be soft underneath. Allow to cool in the pan for 5 minutes, then unmold and transfer to a sheet of waxed paper lightly sprinkled with confectioners' sugar. Cut into bars.

Creamy Lemon Bars

A delicious and luxurious treat, ideal for accompanying a cup of coffee.

Makes 36

❧

INGREDIENTS

*¹/₂ cup confectioners' sugar
1¹/₂ cups all-purpose flour
pinch of salt
³/₄ cup butter, chopped
For the topping
4 eggs
1¹/₂ cups granulated sugar
grated rind of 1 lemon
¹/₂ cup fresh lemon juice
³/₄ cup whipping cream
confectioners' sugar for dusting*

❧

1 Preheat the oven to 325°F. Grease a 13 x 9-inch cake pan. Sift the sugar, flour and salt into a bowl. Rub in the butter until the mixture resembles coarse crumbs.

2 Press the mixture into the bottom of the prepared cake pan. Bake for about 20 minutes, until golden brown.

3 Meanwhile, to make the topping, beat together the eggs and sugar until blended. Add the lemon rind and juice and mix well.

4 Lightly whip the cream and fold into the egg mixture. Pour over the warm crust, return to the oven, and bake for about 40 minutes, until set. Cool completely before cutting into bars. Dust with confectioners' sugar.

Chocolate Raspberry Macaroon Bars

Any seedless preserve, such as strawberry or apricot, can be substituted for raspberry.

Makes 16–18 bars

INGREDIENTS

¹/₂ cup unsalted butter
¹/₂ cup confectioners' sugar
¹/₄ cup cocoa powder
pinch of salt
1 teaspoon almond extract
1¹/₄ cups all-purpose flour
For the topping
scant ¹/₂ cup seedless raspberry
preserves
1 tablespoon raspberry-flavored
liqueur
1 cup mini chocolate chips
1¹/₂ cups finely ground almonds
4 egg whites
pinch of salt
1 cup granulated sugar
¹/₂ teaspoon almond essence
¹/₂ cup slivered almonds

1 Preheat the oven to 325°F. Invert a 9 x 13-inch cake pan. Mold a sheet of foil over the pan and smooth the foil evenly around the corners. Lift off the foil and turn the pan right side up; line with the molded foil. Lightly grease the foil.

2 In a medium bowl, with an electric mixer, beat together the butter, sugar, cocoa and salt until well blended. Add in the almond extract and the flour and mix until the mixture forms a crumbly dough.

3 Turn the dough into the prepared pan and pat firmly over the bottom to make an even layer. Prick the dough with a fork.

4 Bake for 20 minutes, until just set. Remove from the oven and increase the temperature to 375°F.

5 To make the topping, combine the raspberry preserves and raspberry-flavored liqueur in a small bowl. Spread the topping evenly over the chocolate crust, then sprinkle evenly with the chocolate chips.

6 In a food processor fitted with a metal blade, process the almonds, egg whites, salt, sugar and almond extract until well blended and foamy. Gently pour over the jam layer, spreading evenly to the edges of the pan. Sprinkle with slivered almonds.

7 Bake for 20–25 minutes more, until the top is golden and puffed. Transfer to a wire rack to cool in the pan for 20 minutes, until firm.

8 Using the edges of the foil, carefully remove the cake from the pan and cool completely. Peel off the foil and, using a sharp knife, cut into bars.

Lemon Cheese Bars

Makes 24

❧

INGREDIENTS

1 cup all-purpose flour
¹/₂ cup chopped walnuts
¹/₂ cup light brown sugar
¹/₃ cup unsalted butter
grated rind and juice of 1 small
lemon
1 cup full-fat cream cheese
¹/₄ cup granulated sugar
1 tablespoon milk
¹/₂ teaspoon vanilla extract
1 large egg

❧

1 Preheat the oven to 350°F. Grease a 9-inch square cake pan.

2 Beat together the flour, walnuts, brown sugar and butter. Divide the mixture in half. Press one half of the mixture into the prepared cake pan. Bake for 12–15 minutes, until lightly browned. Remove from the oven.

3 Beat together the lemon rind and juice, the cheese and sugar, then beat in the milk, vanilla extract and egg. Spoon over the partly cooked pastry and crumble the remaining mixture evenly over the top. Bake for another 25 minutes, until the top is golden. Transfer to a wire rack to cool, then chill. Cut into bars.

Citrus Spice Bars

Makes 50

❧

INGREDIENTS

¹/₄ cup candied orange peel,
chopped
¹/₃ cup raisins
5 tablespoons rum
3 tablespoons honey
3 tablespoons molasses
1 egg
1 cup ground almonds
1¹/₂ cups whole wheat flour
¹/₂ teaspoon baking powder
large pinch baking soda
1 teaspoon ground cinnamon
¹/₂ teaspoon ground ginger
1 cup unblanched almonds,
chopped
¹/₂ cup sifted confectioners' sugar
about 3 tablespoons orange juice

❧

1 Preheat the oven to 400°F. Lightly grease a 13 x 9-inch cake pan. Place the orange peel, raisins and rum in a bowl, cover and set aside for 1 hour.

2 Pour the honey and molasses into a saucepan and bring to a boil. Set aside to cool, then beat in the egg. Mix together the ground almonds, flour, baking powder, baking soda and spices and stir into the mixture. Stir in the chopped almonds and the rum mixture and form into a dough.

3 Press the dough into the prepared cake pan. Bake for about 20 minutes. Transfer to a wire rack to cool. Sift the confectioners' sugar into a bowl and stir in just enough orange juice to make a spreading consistency. Set aside for 1 hour.

4 Spread the icing over the cake. Decorate if you wish and cut into generous bars.

Chocolate and Coconut Slices

Very simple to make, these slices are deliciously moist and sweet.

Makes 24

❧

INGREDIENTS

*½ cup butter or margarine,
chopped
6 ounces graham crackers,
crushed
4 tablespoons sugar
pinch of salt
1 cup dried coconut
1½ cups semisweet chocolate
chips
1 cup sweetened condensed milk
1 cup chopped walnuts*

❧

1 Preheat the oven to 350°F. Melt the butter or margarine in a small saucepan over low heat.

2 In a bowl, combine the crushed graham crackers, sugar, salt and melted butter or margarine. Press the mixture evenly over the bottom of an ungreased 13 x 9-inch baking dish.

3 Sprinkle the coconut over the cookie base, then sprinkle over the chocolate chips. Pour the condensed milk evenly over the chocolate. Sprinkle the walnuts on top.

4 Bake for 30 minutes. Transfer to a wire rack and allow to cool, preferably overnight. When cooled, cut into slices.

Hermits

Makes 30

INGREDIENTS

³/₄ cup all-purpose flour
1¹/₂ teaspoons baking powder
1 teaspoon ground cinnamon
¹/₂ teaspoon grated nutmeg
¹/₄ teaspoon ground cloves
¹/₄ teaspoon ground allspice
1¹/₂ cups raisins
¹/₂ cup butter or margarine
¹/₂ cup sugar
2 eggs
¹/₂ cup molasses
¹/₂ cup walnuts, chopped

1 Preheat the oven to 350°F. Line the bottom and sides of a 13 x 9-inch pan with waxed paper and grease.

2 Sift together the flour, baking powder and spices into a bowl.

3 Place the raisins in another bowl and toss with a few tablespoons of the flour mixture.

4 With an electric mixer, cream together the butter or margarine and sugar, until light and fluffy. Beat in the eggs, one at a time, then the molasses. Stir in the flour mixture, raisins and walnuts.

5 Spread evenly in the prepared cake pan. Bake for 15–18 minutes, until just set. Leave to cool in the pan before cutting into squares or fingers.

Butterscotch Meringue Bars

Makes 12

INGREDIENTS

4 tablespoons butter
1 cup firmly packed dark brown sugar
1 egg
¹/₂ teaspoon vanilla extract
¹/₂ cup all-purpose flour
pinch of salt
¹/₄ teaspoon grated nutmeg
For the topping
1 egg white
pinch of salt
1 tablespoon light corn syrup
¹/₂ cup granulated sugar
¹/₂ cup walnuts, finely chopped

1 Combine the butter and brown sugar in a saucepan and cook until bubbling. Set aside to cool.

2 Preheat the oven to 350°F. Line an 8-inch square cake pan with waxed paper and grease the paper.

3 Beat the egg and vanilla extract into the cooled sugar mixture. Sift over the flour, salt and nutmeg and fold in. Spread over the bottom of the prepared cake pan.

4 To make the topping, beat the egg white with the salt until it holds soft peaks. Beat in the light corn syrup, then the granulated sugar, and continue beating until the mixture holds stiff peaks.

5 Fold in the nuts and spread on top of the mixture in the pan. Bake for 30 minutes. Cut into bars when cool.

Muffins
and Scones

Muffins are very easy to make and delicious to eat: to mix the batter, simply use a few swift strokes to stir the liquid ingredients, taking no more than 10–20 seconds. This will leave some lumps. Ignore them. If the batter is mixed for too long, the dough will be tough and the muffins will be coarse-textured and full of tunnels. Rather than being mixed to a smooth pouring consistency, the mixture should come off the spoon in coarse dollops.

Muffins are best eaten when freshly made and still warm, certainly on the day of baking. To re-warm muffins, wrap them loosely in foil and heat for approximately 5 minutes in an oven preheated to 450°F.

The distinction between our biscuits and British scones is very slight, although our bakeries, supermarkets and coffee bars do now offer scones as a breakfast biscuit or muffin, to be split and toasted. In Britain, however, they are an essential part of an afternoon tea, eaten while warm, split, spread with butter and served with cream (preferably clotted) and jam.

Whatever the name, the secrets of their perfect, light, tender scones are not making the dough too wet, handling it quickly and very lightly, and rolling it out with even pressure to the correct thickness – at least ³⁄₄ inch, and lastly, preheating the oven to a high temperature, usually about 425°F.

Oatmeal Buttermilk Muffins

Makes 12

❧

INGREDIENTS

1 cup rolled oats
1 cup buttermilk
½ cup butter
½ cup dark brown sugar
1 egg
1 cup all-purpose flour
1 teaspoon baking powder
½ teaspoon baking soda
pinch of salt
¼ cup raisins

❧

Cook's Tip If buttermilk is not available, add 1 teaspoon lemon juice or vinegar to 1 cup of milk. Let the mixture stand a few minutes to curdle before adding it to the oats.

1 In a bowl, combine the oats and buttermilk and allow to soak for 1 hour.

2 Grease 12 muffin pans, or use paper liners. Preheat the oven to 400°F.

3 With an electric mixer, cream the butter and sugar until light and fluffy. Beat in the egg.

4 Sift together the flour, baking powder, baking soda and salt. Stir into the butter mixture, alternating with the oat mixture. Fold in the raisins.

5 Fill the muffin pans two-thirds full. Bake for 20–25 minutes. Transfer to a wire rack to cool.

Pumpkin Muffins

Makes 14

❧

INGREDIENTS

½ cup butter or margarine
¾ cup firmly packed brown sugar
⅓ cup molasses
1 egg, beaten
1 cup cooked or canned pumpkin
1¾ cups all-purpose flour
pinch of salt
1 teaspoon baking soda
1½ teaspoons ground cinnamon
1 teaspoon grated nutmeg
¼ cup currants or raisins

❧

2 With an electric mixer, cream the butter or margarine until soft. Add the sugar and molasses and beat until light and fluffy.

3 Add the egg and pumpkin and stir until well blended.

4 Sift over the flour, salt, baking soda, cinnamon and nutmeg. Fold in until just blended; do not overmix.

5 Fold the currants or raisins into the pumpkin mixture until just evenly combined.

6 Spoon the batter into the prepared muffin pans, filling them two-thirds full.

7 Bake for 12–15 minutes, until the tops spring back when touched lightly. Serve warm or cold.

1 Preheat the oven to 400°F. Grease 14 muffin pans, or use paper liners.

Banana Muffins

Makes 12

❦

INGREDIENTS

2 cups all-purpose flour
1 teaspoon baking powder
1 teaspoon baking soda
pinch of salt
½ teaspoon ground cinnamon
¼ teaspoon grated nutmeg
3 large ripe bananas
1 egg
⅓ cup dark brown sugar
¼ cup vegetable oil
¼ cup raisins

❦

1 Preheat the oven to 375°F.

2 Grease 12 muffin pans, or use paper liners.

3 Sift together the flour, baking powder, baking soda, salt, cinnamon and nutmeg. Set aside.

4 With an electric mixer, mash the peeled bananas at moderate speed.

5 Beat the egg, sugar and oil into the mashed bananas.

6 Add the dry ingredients and beat in gradually, on low speed. Mix until just blended. With a wooden spoon, stir in the raisins. Fill the muffin pans two-thirds full.

7 Bake for 20–25 minutes, until the tops spring back when touched lightly. Transfer to a wire rack to cool.

Maple Pecan Muffins

Makes 20

❧

INGREDIENTS

1¼ cups pecans
2½ cups all-purpose flour
1 teaspoon baking powder
1 teaspoon baking soda
pinch of salt
¼ teaspoon ground cinnamon
½ cup granulated sugar
⅓ cup firmly packed light
brown sugar
3 tablespoons maple syrup
⅔ cup butter
3 eggs
1¼ cups buttermilk
60 pecan halves to decorate

❧

Variation For Pecan Spice Muffins, substitute an equal quantity of molasses for the maple syrup. Increase the cinnamon to ½ teaspoon, and add 1 teaspoon ground ginger and ½ teaspoon grated nutmeg, sifted with the flour and other dry ingredients.

1 Preheat the oven to 350°F. Grease 20 muffin pans, or use paper liners.

2 Spread the pecans on a baking sheet and toast in the oven for 5 minutes. Allow to cool, then chop coarsely and set aside.

3 In a bowl, sift together the flour, baking powder, baking soda, salt and cinnamon. Set aside.

4 In a large mixing bowl, combine the granulated sugar, light brown sugar, maple syrup and butter. Beat with an electric mixer until light and fluffy.

5 Add the eggs, one at a time, beating to incorporate thoroughly after each addition.

6 Pour half of the buttermilk and half of the dry ingredients into the butter mixture, then stir until blended. Repeat with the remaining buttermilk and dry ingredients.

7 Fold the chopped pecans into the batter. Fill the muffin pans two-thirds full. Top with the pecan halves.

8 Bake for 20–25 minutes, until puffed up and golden. Allow to stand for 5 minutes before transferring to a wire rack to cool.

Raspberry Muffins

Low-fat buttermilk gives these muffins a light and spongy texture.

They are delicious to eat at any time of day.

Makes 10–12

❦

INGREDIENTS

2½ cups all-purpose flour
1 tablespoon baking powder
½ cup sugar
1 egg
1 cup buttermilk
4 tablespoons sunflower oil
1 cup raspberries

❦

Variation Cranberry Muffins: a
breakfast treat that is not too sweet.

3 cups all-purpose flour
1 teaspoon baking powder
pinch of salt
½ cup sugar
2 eggs
⅔ cup milk
4 tablespoons corn oil
finely grated rind of 1 orange
1 cup cranberries

1 Preheat the oven to 375°F. Line
12 deep muffin pans with paper
liners. Mix the flour, baking powder,
salt and caster sugar together. Lightly
beat the eggs with the milk and oil.

2 Add the liquids to the dry
ingredients and blend to make a
smooth batter. Divide the mixture
between the muffin pans and bake for
25 minutes, until risen and golden.
Allow to cool in the pans for a few
minutes, and serve warm or cold.

1 Preheat the oven to 400°F.
Arrange 12 paper liners in deep
muffin pans. Sift the flour and
baking powder into a mixing bowl,
stir in the sugar, then make a well
in the center.

2 Mix the egg, buttermilk and
sunflower oil together in a bowl,
pour into the flour mixture and mix
quickly until just combined.

3 Add the raspberries and lightly
fold in with a metal spoon. Spoon
the mixture into the paper liners.

4 Bake for 20–25 minutes, until
golden brown and firm in the
center. Transfer to a wire rack and
serve warm or cold.

Double Chocolate Chip Muffins

These marvelous muffins are packed with chunky semisweet and white chocolate chips.

Makes 16

❦

INGREDIENTS

3½ cups all-purpose flour
1 tablespoon baking powder
2 tablespoons cocoa powder
½ cup firmly packed dark
   brown sugar
2 eggs
⅔ cup sour cream
⅔ cup milk
4 tablespoons sunflower oil
6 ounces white chocolate
6 ounces semisweet chocolate
cocoa powder for dusting

❦

Cook's Tip If sour cream is not available, sour ⅔ cup light cream by stirring in 1 teaspoon lemon juice and letting the mixture stand until thickened.

1 Preheat the oven to 375°F. Place 16 paper muffin liners in muffin pans or popover pans. Sift the flour, baking powder and cocoa into a bowl and stir in the sugar. Make a well in the center.

2 In a separate bowl, beat the eggs with the sour cream, milk and oil, then stir into the well in the dry ingredients. Beat well, gradually incorporating the flour mixture to make a thick and creamy batter.

Variation Make sure you use good quality chocolate with a high cocoa content. Vary the proportions of semisweet and white chocolate, or add in milk chocolate if you prefer.

3 Finely chop the chocolate and stir into the batter mixture.

4 Spoon the mixture into the muffin liners, filling them almost to the top. Bake for 25–30 minutes, until well risen and firm to the touch. Transfer to a wire rack to cool, then dust with cocoa powder.

Chocolate Walnut Muffins

Walnuts and chocolate are a delicious combination.

Makes 12

❦

INGREDIENTS

¾ cup unsalted butter, chopped
5 ounces semisweet chocolate,
chopped
1 cup granulated sugar
¼ cup firmly packed dark
brown sugar
4 eggs
1 teaspoon vanilla extract
¼ teaspoon almond extract
¾ cup all-purpose flour
1 cup walnuts, chopped

❦

1 Preheat the oven to 350°F. Grease muffin pans, or use paper liners.

2 Melt the butter with the chocolate in the top of a double boiler or a heatproof bowl over a saucepan of hot water. Transfer to a large mixing bowl.

3 Stir both the sugars into the chocolate mixture. Mix in the eggs, one at a time, then add the vanilla and almond extract.

4 Sift over the flour and fold in until evenly combined.

5 Stir the walnuts evenly into the chocolate mixture.

6 Fill the muffin pans almost to the top and bake for 30–35 minutes. Allow to stand for 5 minutes before transferring to a wire rack.

Chocolate Chip Muffins

Use the best quality chocolate chips you can find.

Makes 10

❦

INGREDIENTS

½ cup butter or margarine
⅓ cup granulated sugar
2 tablespoons dark brown sugar
2 eggs
1½ cups all-purpose flour
1 teaspoon baking powder
½ cup milk
1 cup semisweet chocolate chips

❦

1 Preheat the oven to 375°F. Grease 10 muffin pans, or use paper liners.

2 With an electric mixer, cream the butter or margarine until soft. Add both sugars and beat until light and fluffy. Beat in the eggs, one at a time.

3 Sift the flour and baking powder, twice. Fold into the butter mixture, alternating with the milk.

4 Divide half of the mixture between the muffin pans. Sprinkle several chocolate chips on top, then cover with a spoonful of batter.

5 Bake for about 25 minutes, until lightly colored. Allow to stand for 5 minutes before transferring to a wire rack to cool.

Banana and Nut Buns

Use walnut pieces instead of pecans if you prefer.

Makes 8

❧

INGREDIENTS

1¼ cups all-purpose flour
1½ teaspoons baking powder
¼ cup butter or margarine
¾ cup sugar
1 egg
1 teaspoon vanilla extract
3 medium bananas, mashed
½ cup chopped pecans
⅓ cup milk

❧

1 Preheat the oven to 375°F. Grease eight muffin pans.

2 Sift the flour and baking powder into a small bowl. Set aside.

3 With an electric mixer, cream together the butter or margarine and the sugar. Add the egg and vanilla extract and beat until fluffy. Mix in the bananas.

4 Add the pecans. With the mixer on low speed, beat in the flour mixture alternately with the milk. Spoon the mixture into the prepared pans. Bake for 20–25 minutes, until a skewer or cake tester inserted in the center of a bun comes out clean.

5 Allow to cool in the muffin pans for 10 minutes. Unmold onto the wire rack. Cool for 10 minutes longer before serving.

Fruit and Cinnamon Buns

Makes 8

❧

INGREDIENTS

1 cup all-purpose flour
1 tablespoon baking powder
pinch of salt
scant ½ cup light brown sugar
1 egg
¾ cup milk
3 tablespoons vegetable oil
2 teaspoons ground cinnamon
1 cup fresh or thawed frozen
blueberries, or black currants

❧

1 Preheat the oven to 375°F. Grease eight muffin pans.

2 With an electric mixer, beat together the first eight ingredients until smooth.

3 Fold the blueberries or black currants into the other ingredients until just evenly combined.

4 Spoon the mixture into the muffin pans, filling them two-thirds full. Bake for about 25 minutes, until a skewer or cake tester inserted in the center of a bun comes out clean.

5 Allow to cool in the muffin pans, on a wire rack, for 10 minutes, then transfer the buns to the wire rack and allow to cool completely.

Carrot Muffins

Makes 12

❦

INGREDIENTS

¾ cup margarine
½ cup dark brown sugar
1 egg
1 tablespoon water
2 cups grated carrots
1¼ cups all-purpose flour
1 teaspoon baking powder
½ teaspoon baking soda
1 teaspoon ground cinnamon
¼ teaspoon grated nutmeg
pinch of salt

❦

1 Preheat the oven to 350°F.
Grease 12 muffin pans, or use
paper liners.

2 With an electric mixer, cream the
margarine and sugar until light
and fluffy. Beat in the egg and water.

3 Stir the grated carrots into the
creamed mixture until evenly
combined. Sift over the flour, baking
powder, baking soda, cinnamon,
nutmeg and salt. Stir to blend evenly.

4 Spoon the batter into the
prepared muffin pans, filling
them almost to the top.

5 Bake for about 35 minutes, until
the tops spring back when
touched lightly. Allow to stand for
10 minutes before transferring to a
wire rack to cool.

Dried Cherry Muffins

If you can't find dried cherries, use the same amount of dried cranberries.

Makes 16

❦

INGREDIENTS

1 cup plain yogurt
1 cup dried cherries
½ cup butter
¾ cup sugar
2 eggs
1 teaspoon vanilla extract
1¾ cups all-purpose flour
2 teaspoons baking powder
1 teaspoon baking soda
pinch of salt

❦

1 In a mixing bowl, combine the
yogurt and cherries. Cover and let
stand for 30 minutes.

2 Preheat the oven to 350°F.
Grease 16 muffin pans, or use
paper liners.

3 With an electric mixer, cream
together the butter and sugar
until light and fluffy.

4 Add the eggs, one at a time,
beating well after each addition.
Add the vanilla extract and the
cherry mixture and stir to blend.
Set aside.

5 In another bowl, sift together the
flour, baking powder, baking
soda and salt. Fold into the cherry
mixture in three batches; do not
overmix.

6 Fill the prepared muffin pans
two-thirds full. Bake for about
20 minutes, until the tops spring back
when touched lightly. Transfer to a
wire rack to cool.

Blueberry Muffins

Makes 12

❧

INGREDIENTS

1¼ cups all-purpose flour
⅓ cup sugar
2 teaspoons baking powder
pinch of salt
2 eggs
4 tablespoons butter, melted
¾ cup milk
1 teaspoon vanilla extract
1 teaspoon grated lemon rind
1 cup fresh blueberries

❧

1 Preheat the oven to 400°F. Grease 12 muffin pans, or use paper liners.

2 Sift the flour, sugar, baking powder and salt into a bowl. Beat the eggs until blended. Stir in the melted butter, milk, vanilla extract and lemon rind.

3 Make a well in the dry ingredients and pour in the egg mixture. With a large metal spoon, stir until the flour is just moistened, not until smooth.

4 Rinse the blueberries and dry well, then gently fold into the batter with a metal spoon, making sure they are distributed evenly.

5 Spoon the batter into the pans, leaving room for the muffins to rise. Bake for 20–25 minutes. Allow to sit for 5 minutes before transferring to a wire rack to cool.

Date and Apple Muffins

These muffins are delicious and very filling.

Makes 12

INGREDIENTS

*1¼ cups self-rising
whole wheat flour
1¼ cups self-rising white flour
1 teaspoon ground cinnamon
1 teaspoon baking powder
2 tablespoons margarine
½ cup firmly packed
light brown sugar
1 eating apple
1 cup apple juice
2 tablespoons pear and apple
spread
1 egg, lightly beaten
½ cup chopped dates
1 tablespoon chopped pecans*

1 Preheat the oven to 400°F. Arrange 12 paper liners in a deep muffin pan. Put the whole wheat flour in a mixing bowl. Sift in the white flour with the cinnamon and baking powder. Rub in the margarine until the mixture resembles bread crumbs, then stir in the brown sugar.

2 Quarter and core the apple, chop the flesh finely and set aside. Stir a little of the apple juice with the fruit spread until smooth. Mix in the remaining juice, then add to the rubbed-in mixture with the beaten egg.

3 Add the chopped apple to the bowl with the dates. Mix quickly until just combined. Divide the mixture among the muffin liners.

4 Sprinkle with the chopped pecans. Bake the muffins for 20–25 minutes, until golden brown and firm in the middle. Transfer to a wire rack and serve while still warm.

Blackberry Muffins

Other berries, such as raspberries or blueberries, can be substituted for the blackberries.

Makes 12

❦

INGREDIENTS

2½ cups all-purpose flour
generous ¼ cup light brown sugar
4 teaspoons baking powder
pinch of salt
generous ½ cup chopped
blanched almonds
generous ½ cup fresh blackberries
2 eggs
⅞ cup milk
4 tablespoons butter, melted
1 tablespoon blackberry liqueur
1 tablespoon rose water

❦

1 Mix the flour, sugar, baking powder and salt in a bowl and stir in the almonds and blackberries, mixing them well to coat with the flour mixture.

2 Preheat the oven to 400°F. Grease 12 muffin pans, or use paper liners.

3 In another bowl, mix the eggs with the milk, then gradually add the butter, liqueur and rose water. Make a well in the center of the bowl of dry ingredients and add the egg and milk mixture. Stir well. Spoon the mixture into the muffin pans or cases. Bake for 20–25 minutes, until browned. Transfer to a wire rack to cool.

Chocolate Blueberry Muffins

Blueberries are one of the many fruits that combine deliciously with chocolate.

Makes 12

❧

INGREDIENTS

½ cup butter
3 ounces semisweet chocolate,
 chopped
generous 1 cup sugar
1 egg, lightly beaten
1 cup buttermilk
2 teaspoons vanilla extract
2½ cups all-purpose flour
1 teaspoon baking soda
generous 1 cup fresh or frozen
 blueberries, thawed
1 ounce semisweet chocolate,
 melted, to decorate

❧

1 Preheat the oven to 375°F. Grease 12 deep muffin pans, or use paper liners. In a medium saucepan over a medium heat, melt the butter and chocolate until smooth, stirring frequently. Remove from the heat and allow to cool slightly.

2 Stir in the sugar, egg, buttermilk and vanilla extract. Gently fold in the flour and baking soda until just blended. (Do not overblend, although the mixture may be lumpy with some unblended flour.) Fold in the berries.

3 Spoon the batter into the prepared pans, filling to the top. Bake for 25–30 minutes, until a skewer or cake tester inserted in the center comes out with just a few crumbs attached. Remove the muffins in their paper liners to a wire rack immediately (if left in the pan they will get soggy). To decorate, drizzle with the melted chocolate and serve warm or cool.

Prune Muffins

Muffins with prunes are moist, delicious breakfast treats.

Makes 12

❧

INGREDIENTS

1 egg
1 cup milk
¼ cup vegetable oil
¼ cup granulated sugar
2 tablespoons dark brown sugar
2 cups all-purpose flour
2 teaspoons baking powder
pinch of salt
¼ teaspoon grated nutmeg
¾ cup cooked pitted prunes, chopped

❧

1 Preheat the oven to 400°F. Grease 12 muffin pans or use paper liners.

2 Break the egg into a mixing bowl and beat with a fork. Beat in the milk and oil.

3 Stir the sugars into the egg mixture. Set aside. Sift the flour, baking powder, salt and nutmeg into a mixing bowl. Make a well in the center, pour in the egg mixture and stir. The batter should be slightly lumpy.

4 Gently fold the prunes into the batter until just evenly distributed. Fill the prepared muffin pans two-thirds full.

5 Bake for about 20 minutes, until golden brown. Allow to stand for 10 minutes before transferring to a wire rack. Serve warm or at room temperature.

Yogurt Honey Muffins

Makes 12

❧

INGREDIENTS

4 tablespoons butter
5 tablespoons honey
1 cup plain yogurt
1 egg
grated rind of 1 lemon
¼ cup lemon juice
1 cup all-purpose flour
1 cup whole wheat flour
1½ teaspoons baking soda
pinch of grated nutmeg

❧

Variation For Walnut Yogurt Honey Muffins, add ½ cup chopped walnuts, folded in with the flour. This makes a more substantial muffin.

1 Preheat the oven to 375°F. Grease 12 muffin pans, or use paper liners.

2 In a saucepan, melt the butter and honey. Remove from the heat and set aside to cool slightly.

3 In a bowl, beat together the yogurt, egg, lemon rind and juice. Add the butter and honey mixture. Set aside.

4 In another bowl, sift together the dry ingredients. Fold the dry ingredients into the yogurt mixture just to blend.

5 Fill the prepared muffin pans two-thirds full. Bake for 20–25 minutes, until the tops spring back when touched lightly. Allow to cool in the pan for 5 minutes before transferring to a wire rack. Serve warm or at room temperature.

Raisin Bran Muffins

Makes 15

❦

INGREDIENTS

4 tablespoons butter or margarine
⅔ cup all-purpose flour
½ cup whole wheat flour
1½ teaspoons baking soda
pinch of salt
1 teaspoon ground cinnamon
½ cup bran
½ cup raisins
⅓ cup dark brown sugar
¼ cup granulated sugar
1 egg
1 cup buttermilk
juice of ½ lemon

❦

1 Preheat the oven to 400°F. Grease 15 muffin pans, or use paper liners.

2 Place the butter or margarine in a saucepan and melt over low heat. Set aside. In a mixing bowl, sift together the all-purpose flour, whole wheat flour, baking soda, salt and cinnamon.

3 Add the bran, raisins and sugars and stir until blended. In another bowl, mix together the egg, buttermilk, lemon juice and melted butter or margarine.

4 Add the buttermilk mixture to the dry ingredients and stir lightly and quickly until just moistened; do not mix until smooth.

5 Spoon the batter into the prepared muffin pans, filling them almost to the top. Bake for 15–20 minutes, until golden. Serve warm or at room temperature.

Raspberry Crumble Muffins

Makes 12

INGREDIENTS

1½ cups all-purpose flour
2 teaspoons baking powder
pinch of salt
1 teaspoon ground cinnamon
¼ cup granulated sugar
¼ cup firmly packed light
brown sugar
½ cup butter, melted
1 egg
½ cup milk
1¼ cups fresh raspberries
grated rind of 1 lemon
For the crumble topping
¼ cup pecans, finely chopped
¼ cup firmly packed
dark brown sugar
3 tablespoons all-purpose flour
1 teaspoon ground cinnamon
3 tablespoons butter, melted

1 Preheat the oven to 350°F. Grease 12 muffin pans, or use paper liners. Sift the flour, baking powder, salt and cinnamon into a bowl. Add the sugars, and stir to blend.

2 Make a well in the center of the mixture. Place the butter, egg and milk in the well and mix until just combined. Stir in the raspberries and lemon rind. Spoon the batter into the prepared muffin pans, filling them almost to the top.

3 To make the crumble topping, mix the pecans, dark brown sugar, flour and cinnamon in a bowl. Stir in the melted butter.

4 Spoon some of the crumble over each muffin. Bake for about 25 minutes. Transfer to a wire rack to cool slightly. Serve warm.

Nutty Muffins with Walnut Liqueur

Walnut liqueur gives a lift to these big crunchy muffins.

Makes 12–14

INGREDIENTS

2 cups all-purpose flour
4 teaspoons baking powder
½ teaspoon apple pie spice
pinch of salt
⅔ cup firmly packed light
brown sugar
¾ cup chopped walnuts
4 tablespoons butter, melted
2 eggs
¾ cup milk
2 tablespoons walnut liqueur
For the topping
2 tablespoons dark brown sugar
¼ cup chopped walnuts

1 Preheat the oven to 400°F. Grease 12–14 muffin pans or deep bun pans, or use paper muffin liners supported in muffin pans. Sift the flour, baking powder, apple pie spice and salt into a mixing bowl, then stir in the sugar and chopped walnuts.

2 In a cup, combine the melted butter, eggs, milk and liqueur.

3 Pour the butter mixture into the dry mixture and stir for just long enough to combine the ingredients. The batter should be lumpy.

4 Fill the muffin or bun pans two-thirds full, then top with a sprinkling of dark brown sugar and walnuts. Bake for 15 minutes, until the muffins are golden brown. Leave in the pans for a few minutes, then transfer to a wire rack to cool.

Apple and Cinnamon Muffins

These spicy muffins are quick and easy to make and are perfect for serving for a special breakfast.

Makes 6

❦

INGREDIENTS

1 egg, beaten
3 tablespoons granulated sugar
½ cup milk
¼ cup butter, melted
1¼ cups all-purpose flour
1½ teaspoons baking powder
pinch of salt
½ teaspoon ground cinnamon
2 small eating apples, peeled,
cored and finely chopped
For the topping
3 tablespoons raw sugar
1 teaspoon ground cinnamon

❦

Cook's Tip Do not overmix the muffin mixture – it should be lumpy.

3 Bake for 30–35 minutes, until well risen and golden. Transfer to a wire rack to cool.

1 Preheat the oven to 400°F. Line six large muffin pans with paper liners. Mix the egg, sugar, milk and melted butter in a large bowl. Sift in the flour, baking powder, salt and cinnamon. Add the chopped apple and mix coarsely.

2 Spoon the mixture into the prepared muffin pans. To make the topping, mix the raw sugar with the cinnamon. Sprinkle over the uncooked muffins. Bake for 30–35 minutes, until well risen and golden. Transfer to a wire rack to cool.

Pineapple and Cinnamon Pancakes

Making the batter with pineapple juice instead of milk cuts down on fat and adds to the taste.

Makes 24

INGREDIENTS

1 cup self-rising whole wheat flour
1 cup self-rising white flour
1 teaspoon ground cinnamon
1 tablespoon sugar
1 egg
1¼ cups pineapple juice
½ cup dried pineapple, chopped

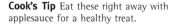

Cook's Tip Eat these right away with applesauce for a healthy treat.

1 Preheat a griddle, heavy-bottomed frying pan or an electric frying pan. Put the whole wheat flour in a mixing bowl. Sift in the white flour, add the cinnamon and sugar and make a well in the center. Add the egg with half of the pineapple juice.

2 Gradually incorporate the flour to make a smooth batter. Beat in the remaining juice with the chopped pineapple.

3 Grease the griddle or pan. Drop tablespoons of the batter onto the surface, leaving them until they bubble and the bubbles begin to burst.

4 Turn the drop pancakes with a metal spatula and cook until the underside is golden brown. Continue to cook in successive batches.

Chocolate Chip Banana Pancakes

These delicious moist pancakes are topped with cream and toasted almonds.

Makes 16

INGREDIENTS

2 ripe bananas
⅞ cup milk
2 eggs
1¼ cups self-rising flour
¼ cup ground almonds
1 tablespoon granulated sugar
pinch of salt
1½ tablespoons semisweet
chocolate chips
butter for frying
For the topping
⅔ cup whipping cream
1 tablespoon confectioners' sugar
½ cup toasted slivered almonds,
to decorate

Cook's Tip For banana and blueberry pancakes, replace the chocolate with 1 cup fresh blueberries. These pancakes are also delicious when accompanied by ice cream.

1 In a bowl, mash the bananas with a fork, combine with half of the milk and beat in the eggs. Sift in the flour, ground almonds, sugar and salt. Make a well in the center and pour in the remaining milk. Add the chocolate chips and stir to produce a thick batter.

2 Heat one pat of butter in a non-stick frying pan. Spoon the pancake mixture into heaps, allowing room for them to spread. When the mixture starts to bubble, turn the pancakes over and cook briefly on the other side.

3 Lightly whip the cream with the confectioners' sugar to sweeten it. Spoon the cream onto the pancakes and decorate with slivered almonds.

Teatime Scones

Makes 16

❧

INGREDIENTS

2 cups all-purpose flour
pinch of salt
½ teaspoon baking soda
1 teaspoon cream of tartar
2 tablespoons butter
about ⅔ cup milk or buttermilk

❧

Variation These traditional favorites can be varied by adding:
1–2 tablespoons of chocolate chips or 1–2 teaspoons ground cinnamon.

1 Preheat the oven to 425°F. Flour a baking sheet. Sift the flour, salt, baking soda and cream of tartar into a bowl.

2 Rub in the fat until the mixture resembles fine bread crumbs. Gradually stir in just enough milk to make a light, spongy dough.

3 Turn the dough onto a lightly floured surface and knead until smooth. Roll to 1 inch thick. Cut into rounds with a floured 2-inch cutter (or a 1½-inch cutter for cocktail savories).

4 Place the scones on the prepared baking sheet and brush the tops with milk. Bake for 7–10 minutes, until the scones are well risen and golden brown.

Lavender Scones

Serve these scented scones warm, with plum jam and whipped cream.

Makes 12

❧

INGREDIENTS

2 cups all-purpose flour
1 tablespoon baking powder
4 tablespoons butter
¼ cup sugar
2 teaspoons fresh lavender florets
or 1 teaspoon dried culinary
lavender, roughly chopped
about ¾ cup milk

❧

1 Preheat the oven to 425°F. Grease a baking sheet. Sift together the flour and baking powder. Rub the butter into the dry ingredients until the mixture resembles bread crumbs.

2 Stir in the sugar and lavender florets, reserving a pinch of lavender to sprinkle on the top of the scones before baking them.

3 Add enough milk to make a soft, sticky dough. Pull the mixture together and then turn the dough onto a well-floured work surface.

4 Shape the dough into a circle, and roll out to a 1 inch depth. Using a floured cutter, stamp out 12 scones.

5 Place on the prepared baking sheet. Brush the tops with a little milk and sprinkle with the reserved lavender.

6 Bake for 10–12 minutes, until golden.

Sunflower Golden Raisin Biscuits

Makes 10–12

❧

INGREDIENTS

2 cups self-rising flour
1 teaspoon baking powder
2 tablespoons margarine
2 tablespoons raw sugar
⅓ cup golden raisins
2 tablespoons sunflower seeds
⅔ cup plain yogurt
about 2–3 tablespoons milk

❧

1 Preheat the oven to 450°F. Lightly oil a baking sheet. Sift the flour and baking powder into a bowl and rub in the margarine. Stir in the sugar, golden raisins and half of the sunflower seeds, then mix in the plain yogurt.

2 Add just enough milk to the mixture to make a soft dough.

3 Roll out on a lightly floured surface to about ¾ inch thick. Cut into 2½-inch rounds with a floured cutter and lift onto the baking sheet.

4 Brush the biscuits with milk and sprinkle them with the reserved sunflower seeds.

5 Bake for 10–12 minutes, until well risen and golden brown. Transfer to a cooling rack. Serve while still warm, with jam, butter or low-fat spread.

Whole Wheat Scones

Whole wheat scones are both delicious and healthy.

Makes 16

❧

INGREDIENTS

¾ cup cold butter
2 cups whole wheat flour
1 cup all-purpose flour
2 tablespoons sugar
pinch of salt
2½ teaspoons baking soda
2 eggs
¾ cup buttermilk
¼ cup raisins

❧

1 Preheat the oven to 400°F. Grease and flour a large baking sheet.

2 Cut the butter into small pieces. Combine the dry ingredients in a bowl. Add the butter and rub in until the mixture resembles coarse crumbs. Set aside.

3 In another bowl, beat together the eggs and buttermilk. Set aside 2 tablespoons for glazing.

4 Stir the remaining egg mixture into the dry ingredients until it just holds together. Stir in the raisins.

5 Roll out the dough about ¾ inch thick. Stamp out circles with a floured cookie cutter. Place on the prepared baking sheet and brush with the glaze.

6 Bake for 12–15 minutes, until golden. Allow to cool slightly before serving. Split in half with a fork while still warm and spread with butter and jam, if wished.

Orange Raisin Scones

Makes 16

❧

INGREDIENTS

2 cups all-purpose flour
1½ tablespoons baking powder
⅓ cup sugar
pinch of salt
5 tablespoons butter, chopped
grated rind of 1 large orange
⅓ cup raisins
½ cup buttermilk
milk for glazing

❧

1 Preheat the oven to 425°F. Grease and flour a large baking sheet.

2 Combine the dry ingredients in a large bowl. Add the butter and rub in until the mixture resembles coarse crumbs.

3 Add the orange rind and raisins. Gradually stir in the buttermilk to form a soft dough.

4 Roll out the dough on a floured surface to about ¾ inch thick. Stamp out circles with a floured cookie cutter.

5 Place on the prepared baking sheet and brush the tops with milk. Bake for 12–15 minutes, until golden. Serve hot or warm, with butter or whipped cream, and jam.

Cook's Tip For light, delicate scones, handle the dough as little as possible. If you wish, split the scones when cool and toast them. Butter them while they are still hot.

Cookies
for Kids

This chapter includes recipes that are suitable for children to eat, like Gingerbread Teddy Bears, and recipes that children can make themselves. Quite a number of these recipes do not even need to be baked, such as Date Crunch, Fruit and Nut Clusters and Marshmallow Krispie Cakes.

Kids — before you embark on a cookie-making session, there are a few guidelines that will help you towards ending up with a batch to be proud of. Start by washing and drying your hands. If your hair is long, tie it back. Wear an apron both to protect your clothes from the food and to protect the food from your clothes. Make sure the kitchen surfaces are clean and tidy before you begin.

Next, read through the recipe from start to finish very carefully so you can make sure you have all the ingredients and equipment you will need, and so you have a clear idea of what you are going to be doing and in what order. Now you can get out all the equipment you'll need and assemble and carefully measure all the ingredients.

Follow the recipe exactly and take your time. Avoid any distractions or interruptions, such as friends or brothers or sisters coming in, or the radio playing, in case you make a mistake or forget where you are in the recipe. If you are in any doubt about anything at all, at any time, or feel you need a hand, don't hesitate to ask a grown-up.

Chewy Fruit Muesli Slice

An easy recipe that needs just measuring, mixing and baking.

Makes 8

INGREDIENTS

½ cup dried apricots, chopped
1 eating apple, cored and grated
1¼ cups Swiss-style muesli
⅔ cup apple juice
1 tablespoon soft margarine

1 Preheat the oven to 375°F. Place all the ingredients in a large bowl and mix well.

2 Press the mixture into an 8-inch nonstick cake pan and bake for 35–40 minutes, until lightly browned and firm.

3 Mark the muesli slice into eight wedges and allow to cool in the pan.

Oat and Apricot Clusters

Here is a variation on an old favorite that children can easily make themselves,
so have plenty of the dried fruits and nuts ready for them to add.

Makes 12

INGREDIENTS

4 tablespoons butter or margarine
3 tablespoons honey
½ cup rolled oats
⅓ cup chopped dried apricots
1 tablespoon dried banana chips
1 tablespoon dried
shredded coconut
2–3 cups cornflakes or Rice
Krispies

1 Place the butter or margarine and honey in a small saucepan and warm over low heat, stirring.

2 Add the oats, apricots, banana chips, coconut and cornflakes or Rice Krispies and mix well.

3 Spoon the mixture into 12 paper baking liners, piling it up roughly. Transfer to a baking sheet, or a tray, and chill until set and firm.

Cook's Tip The ingredients can be changed according to what's in your pantry – try peanuts, pecans, raisins or dates.

Fruit and Nut Clusters

This is a fun, no-cook recipe that children will like to make and eat.

Makes 24

INGREDIENTS

8 ounces white chocolate
⅓ cup sunflower seeds
½ cup slivered almonds
⅓ cup sesame seeds
⅓ cup raisins
1 teaspoon ground cinnamon

1 Break the white chocolate into small pieces. Put the chocolate into a heatproof bowl over a saucepan of hot water on low heat. Do not allow the water to touch the base of the bowl, or the chocolate may become too hot.

2 Alternatively, put the chocolate in a microwave-proof container and heat it on Medium for 3 minutes. Stir the melted chocolate until it is smooth and glossy.

3 Mix the remaining ingredients together, pour in the chocolate and stir well.

4 Using a teaspoon, spoon the mixture into paper baking liners and allow to set.

Marshmallow Krispie Cakes

Makes 45

❧

INGREDIENTS

9 ounce bag of toffees
4 tablespoons butter
3 tablespoons milk
1 cup marshmallows
6 cups Rice Krispies

❧

1 Lightly brush an 8 x 13-inch roasting pan with a little oil. Put the toffees, butter and milk in a saucepan and heat gently, stirring until the toffees have melted.

2 Add the marshmallows and cereal, and stir until well mixed and the marshmallows have melted.

3 Spoon into the prepared roasting pan, level the surface and allow to set. Cut into squares, put into paper baking liners and serve.

4 When cool and hard, cut into squares, remove from the pan, and put into paper cases to serve.

Date Crunch

Makes 24

INGREDIENTS

8-ounce package graham crackers
⅓ cup butter
2 tablespoons light corn syrup
½ cup pitted dates, finely chopped
3 ounces golden raisins
5 ounces milk or semisweet
chocolate, chopped

Cook's Tip For an alternative topping, drizzle 3 ounces melted white and 3 ounces melted dark chocolate over.

1 Line a 7-inch square shallow cake pan with foil. Put the crackers in a plastic bag and crush coarsely with a rolling pin.

2 Gently heat the butter and syrup in a small saucepan until the butter has melted.

3 Stir in the crushed crackers, the dates and golden raisins and mix well. Spoon into the prepared pan, press flat with the back of a spoon and chill for 1 hour.

4 Melt the chocolate in a heatproof bowl, over a saucepan of hot water, stirring until smooth. Spoon over the cookie mixture, spreading evenly with a spatula. Chill until set. Lift the foil out of the cake pan and peel away. Cut the crunch into 24 pieces and arrange on a plate.

Peanut Cookies

Packing up a picnic? Got a birthday party coming up?
Make sure some of these nutty cookies are on the menu.

Makes 25

❧

INGREDIENTS

1 cup butter
*2 tablespoons smooth peanut
butter*
1 cup confectioners' sugar
½ cup cornstarch
2 cups all-purpose flour
1 cup unsalted peanuts

❧

1 Put the butter and peanut butter in a bowl and beat together. Add the confectioners' sugar, cornstarch and all-purpose flour and mix together to make a soft dough.

2 Preheat the oven to 350°F. Lightly oil two baking sheets. Roll the mixture into 25 small balls, using your hands, and place on the baking sheets. Leave plenty of room for the cookies to spread.

3 Press the tops of the balls of dough flat, using either the back of a fork or your fingertips.

4 Press a few of the peanuts into each of the cookies. Bake for 15–20 minutes, until lightly browned. Allow to cool for a few minutes before lifting them carefully onto a wire rack with a metal spatula.

Cook's Tip Make monster cookies by rolling bigger balls of dough. Remember to leave plenty of room on the baking sheets for them to spread, though.

Chocolate Crackle-Tops

Older children will enjoy making these distinctive cookies.

Makes 38

INGREDIENTS

*7 ounces semisweet chocolate,
chopped
scant ½ cup unsalted butter
½ cup granulated sugar
3 eggs
1 teaspoon vanilla extract
scant 2 cups all-purpose flour
¼ cup unsweetened cocoa
½ teaspoon baking powder
pinch of salt
1½ cups confectioners' sugar for
coating*

1 In a medium saucepan over low heat, melt the chocolate and butter together until smooth, stirring frequently.

2 Remove from the heat. Stir in the sugar, and continue stirring for 2–3 minutes, until the sugar dissolves. Add the eggs one at a time, beating well after each addition; stir in the vanilla.

3 Into a bowl, sift together the flour, cocoa, baking powder and salt. Gradually stir into the chocolate mixture in batches, until just blended.

4 Cover the dough and refrigerate for at least 1 hour, until the dough is cold and holds its shape.

5 Preheat the oven to 325°F. Grease two or more large baking sheets. Place the confectioners' sugar in a small, deep bowl. Using a small ice-cream scoop or round teaspoon, scoop cold dough into small balls and, between the palms of your hands, roll into 1½ inch balls.

6 Drop each ball into the confectioners' sugar and roll until heavily coated. Remove with a slotted spoon and tap against the side of the bowl to remove excess sugar. Place on the prepared baking sheets 1½ inches apart.

7 Bake the cookies for 10– 15 minutes, until the tops feel slightly firm when touched. Remove the baking sheet to a wire rack for 2–3 minutes. With a metal spatula, remove the cookies to a wire rack to cool completely.

Chocolate Dominoes

A recipe for children to eat rather than make. Ideal for birthday parties.

Makes 16

❧

INGREDIENTS

¾ cup soft margarine
¾ cup granulated sugar
1¼ cups self-rising flour
¼ cup cocoa powder, sifted
3 eggs
For the topping
¾ cup butter
¼ cup cocoa powder
2½ cups confectioners' sugar
a few licorice strips and 4-ounce
package M & M's, for decoration

❧

Variation To make Traffic Light Cakes, omit the cocoa and add an extra 3 tablespoons all-purpose flour. Omit cocoa from the icing and add an extra 4 tablespoons confectioners' sugar and ½ teaspoon vanilla extract. Spread over the cakes and decorate with red, yellow and green candied cherries to look like traffic lights.

1 Preheat the oven to 350°F. Lightly brush a 7 x 11-inch baking pan with a little oil and line the base of the pan with waxed paper.

2 Put all the cake ingredients in a bowl and beat until smooth.

3 Spoon into the prepared cake pan and level the surface with a spatula.

4 Bake for 30 minutes, until the cake springs back when pressed with the fingertips.

5 Cool in the pan for 5 minutes, then loosen the edges with a knife and transfer to a wire rack. Peel off the paper and allow the cake to cool. Turn the cake onto a chopping board and cut into 16 bars.

6 To make the topping, place the butter in a bowl, sift in the cocoa and confectioners' sugar and beat until smooth. Spread the topping evenly over the cakes with a spatula.

7 Add a strip of licorice to each cake, decorate with M & M's for domino dots and arrange the cakes on a serving plate.

Lemony Peanut Pairs

For those who don't like peanut butter, use buttercream or chocolate-and-nut spread instead.

Makes 8–10

❦

INGREDIENTS

¼ cup light brown sugar
¼ cup soft margarine
1 teaspoon grated lemon rind
¾ cup whole wheat flour
¼ cup chopped crystallized
    pineapple
2 tablespoons smooth peanut
    butter
sifted confectioners' sugar for
    dusting

❦

1 Preheat the oven to 375°F.
Grease a baking sheet. Cream the
sugar, margarine and lemon rind
together. Work in the flour and knead
until smooth.

2 Roll out thinly and cut into
rounds, then place on the baking
sheet. Press on pieces of pineapple
and bake for 15–20 minutes. Cool.
Sandwich together with peanut
butter, dust with confectioners' sugar.

Ginger Cookies

*If your children enjoy cooking with you, mixing and rolling the dough, or cutting out
different shapes, this is the ideal recipe to let them practice on.*

Makes 16

❦

INGREDIENTS

⅔ cup brown sugar
½ cup soft margarine
pinch of salt
few drops of vanilla extract
1¼ cups whole wheat flour
1 tablespoon cocoa, sifted
2 teaspoons ground ginger
a little milk
icing glaze and candied cherries,
    to decorate

❦

1 Preheat the oven to 375°F. Grease
a baking sheet. Cream together
the sugar, margarine, salt and vanilla
extract until very soft and light.

2 Work in the flour, cocoa and
ginger, adding a little milk, if
necessary, to bind the mixture.
Knead lightly on a floured surface
until smooth.

3 Roll out the dough to about
¼ inch thick. Stamp out shapes
using floured cookie cutters and place
on the prepared baking sheet.

4 Bake the cookies for 10–15
minutes. Allow to cool on the
baking sheets until firm, then transfer
to a wire rack to cool completely.
Decorate with glaze icing and
candied cherries.

Gingerbread Jungle

Snappy cookies in animal shapes, which can be decorated in your own style.

Makes 14

❧

INGREDIENTS

1½ cups self-rising flour
½ teaspoon baking soda
½ teaspoon ground cinnamon
2 teaspoons granulated sugar
¼ cup butter
3 tablespoons light corn syrup
½ cup confectioners' sugar
1–2 teaspoons water

❧

Cook's Tip Any cutters can be used with the same mixture. Obviously, the smaller the cutters, the more cookies you will make.

1 Preheat the oven to 375°F. Lightly oil two baking sheets.

2 Put the flour, baking soda, cinnamon and granulated sugar in a bowl and mix together. Melt the butter and syrup in a saucepan. Pour over the dry ingredients.

3 Mix together well and then use your hands to pull the mixture together to make a dough.

4 Turn onto a lightly floured surface and roll out to about ¼ inch thick.

5 Use floured animal cutters to cut shapes from the dough and arrange on the prepared baking sheets, leaving enough room between them to rise.

6 Press the trimmings back into a ball, roll it out and cut more shapes. Continue until all the dough is used. Bake for 8–12 minutes, until lightly browned.

7 Allow to cool slightly, before transferring to a wire rack with a metal spatula. Sift the confectioners' sugar into a small bowl and add enough water to make a fairly soft icing.

8 Spoon the icing into a pastry bag fitted with a small, plain nozzle and pipe decorations on the cookies.

Sweet Necklaces

These are too complicated for young children to make but are ideal as novelty Christmas presents. Arrange in a pretty, tissue-lined box or tin for presentation.

Makes 12

INGREDIENTS

*1 quantity Lebkuchen mixture
1 quantity icing glaze
pink food coloring
selection of small candies
6 yards fine pink, blue or white
ribbon*

1 Preheat the oven to 350°F. Grease two large baking sheets. Roll out slightly more than half of the Lebkuchen mixture on a lightly floured surface to a thickness of ¼ inch.

3 Gather the trimmings together with the remaining dough. Roll the dough under the palms of your hands, to make a thick sausage about 1 inch in diameter. Cut in ½-inch slices. Using the skewer, make a hole in the center of each. Put on the second baking sheet.

5 Put half the icing glaze in a paper icing bag and snip off a tip. Use to pipe outlines around the stars. Color the remaining icing with the pink coloring. Spoon into a paper icing bag fitted with a star nozzle.

6 Cut the candies into smaller pieces and use to decorate the cookies. Set aside to harden.

4 Bake for about 8 minutes, until slightly risen and just beginning to color. Remove from the oven and, while still warm, re-make the skewer holes because the gingerbread will have spread slightly during baking. Allow to cool on a wire rack.

2 Cut out stars using a floured 1-inch star cutter. Transfer to a baking sheet, spacing them evenly. Taking care not to distort the shape of the stars, make a large hole in the center of each, using a metal or wooden skewer.

7 Cut the ribbon into 20-inch lengths. Thread a selection of the cookies onto each ribbon.

Chocolate-Tipped Cookies

Get those cold hands wrapped around a steaming hot drink,

and tuck into chocolate-tipped cookies.

Makes 22

❦

INGREDIENTS

½ cup margarine
3 tablespoons confectioners'
sugar, sifted
1¼ cups all-purpose flour
few drops vanilla extract
3 ounces semisweet chocolate,
chopped

1 Preheat the oven to 350°F. Lightly grease two baking sheets. Put the margarine and confectioners' sugar in a bowl and cream them together until very soft. Mix in the flour and vanilla extract.

2 Spoon the mixture into a large pastry bag fitted with a large star nozzle and pipe 4–5 inch lines on the prepared baking sheets. Cook for 15–20 minutes, until pale golden brown. Allow to cool slightly before lifting onto a wire rack. Let the cookies cool completely.

3 Put the chocolate in a small heatproof bowl. Stand in a saucepan of hot, but not boiling, water until it melts. Dip both ends of each cookie into the chocolate, put back on the rack and allow to set. Serve with hot chocolate topped with whipped cream.

Cook's Tip Make round cookies if you prefer, and dip half of each cookie in the melted chocolate.

Five-Spice Fingers

Light, crumbly cookies with an unusual Chinese five-spice flavoring.

Makes 28

❧

INGREDIENTS

½ cup margarine
½ cup confectioners' sugar
1 cup all-purpose flour
2 teaspoons Chinese five-spice
powder
grated rind and juice of ½ orange

❧

1 Preheat the oven to 350°F. Lightly grease two baking sheets. Put the margarine and half the confectioners' sugar in a bowl and beat with a wooden spoon, until the mixture is smooth and creamy.

2 Add the flour and five-spice powder and beat again. Spoon the mixture into a large pastry bag fitted with a large star nozzle.

3 Pipe short lines of mixture, about 3 inches long, on the prepared baking sheets. Leave enough room for them to spread.

4 Bake for 15 minutes, until lightly brown. Allow to cool slightly, before transferring to a wire rack with a metal spatula.

5 Sift the remaining confectioners' sugar into a small bowl and stir in the orange rind. Add enough juice to make a thin icing. Brush over the cookies while they are still warm.

Cook's Tip These cookies are delicious served with ice cream or creamy desserts.

Gingerbread Teddy Bears

These endearing teddy bears, dressed in striped pajamas, would make a perfect gift for friends of any age. If you can't get a large cutter, make smaller bears or use a traditional gingerbread-man cutter. You might need some help from an adult with the decorating.

Makes 6

INGREDIENTS

3 ounces white chocolate, chopped
6 ounces ready-to-roll white sugar
paste
blue food coloring
1 ounce semisweet or milk
chocolate
For the gingerbread
1½ cups all-purpose flour
¼ teaspoon baking soda
pinch of salt
1 teaspoon ground ginger
1 teaspoon ground cinnamon
⅓ cup unsalted butter, chopped
⅓ cup sugar
2 tablespoons maple or corn syrup
1 egg yolk, beaten

1 To make the gingerbread, sift together the flour, baking soda, salt and spices into a large bowl. Rub the butter into the flour until the mixture resembles fine bread crumbs.

2 Stir in the sugar, syrup and egg yolk and mix to a firm dough. Knead lightly. Wrap and chill for 30 minutes.

3 Preheat the oven to 350°F. Grease two large baking sheets. Roll out the gingerbread dough on a floured surface and cut out teddy bears, using a floured 5-inch cookie cutter.

4 Transfer to the prepared baking sheets and bake for 10–15 minutes, until just beginning to color around the edges. Leave on the baking sheets for 3 minutes and then transfer to a wire rack.

5 Melt half of the white chocolate. Put in a paper icing bag and snip off the tip. Make a neat template for the bears' clothes: draw an outline of the cutter onto paper, finishing at the neck, halfway down the arms and around the legs.

6 Thinly roll the sugar paste on a surface dusted with confectioners' sugar. Use the template to cut out the clothes, and secure them to the bears with the melted chocolate.

7 Use the sugar paste trimmings to add ears, eyes and snouts. Dilute the blue coloring with a little water and use it to paint the striped pajamas.

8 Melt the remaining white chocolate and the plain or milk chocolate in separate bowls over saucepans of hot water. Put in separate paper piping bags and snip off the tips. Use the white chocolate to pipe a decorative outline around the pajamas and use the semisweet or milk chocolate to pipe the faces.

Cookie
Treats
and Gifts

Everyone has times when they feel the need to indulge themselves. If your fancy is for something rich and sweet, or if you want to give someone a treat, delve into the next few pages and you will find just the ticket.

A delicious gift that is homemade is always received with delight, and cookies, because they have a special place in nearly everyone's heart, are doubly acceptable, even if they are simple. Of course, if the cookies require a little extra skill, such as Honey and Nut Clusters, they will be

received with even more pleasure. With homemade cookies, it is so easy to hit upon an ideal gift every time, whether it is just a small token or something very special.

The slightly more complicated cookies are also particularly therapeutic to make and provide a rewarding job for a quiet morning or afternoon, or a rainy day when you want to bring a little sunshine into your life. However, none of the recipes in this chapter are beyond the bounds of a reasonably competent home cook.

Chocolate Nut Clusters

These are an ideal way to end a dinner party, or to give as a gift for a special friend.

Makes 30

❧

INGREDIENTS

2¹/₄ cups heavy cream
2 tablespoons unsalted butter,
chopped
1¹/₂ cups light corn syrup
scant 1 cup granulated sugar
¹/₂ cup firmly packed light
brown sugar
pinch of salt
1 tablespoon vanilla extract
3¹/₄ cups hazelnuts, pecans,
walnuts, brazil nuts or unsalted
peanuts, or a combination
14 ounces semisweet chocolate,
chopped
2 tablespoons vegetable shortening

❧

2 Place the bottom of the saucepan in a pan of cold water to stop cooking, or transfer the caramel to a smaller saucepan. Cool slightly, then stir in the vanilla extract.

3 Stir the nuts into the caramel until well-coated. Using an oiled tablespoon, drop spoonfuls of the nut mixture onto the prepared sheets, about 1 inch apart. If the mixture hardens, return to the heat to soften.

1 Lightly oil two baking sheets. In a heavy-bottomed saucepan over medium heat, cook the first six ingredients until the sugars dissolve and the butter melts. Bring to a boil and cook, stirring frequently, for about 1 hour, until the caramel reaches 238°F (soft ball stage) on a sugar thermometer.

4 Refrigerate the clusters for 30 minutes, until firm and cold, or leave in a cool place until hardened.

Cook's Tip If you do not have a sugar thermometer, you can test cooked sugar for "soft ball stage" by spooning a small amount into a bowl of cold water: when taken out it should form a soft ball when rolled between finger and thumb.

5 Using a metal palette knife, transfer the clusters to a wire rack placed over a baking sheet to catch drips.

6 In a medium saucepan, over a low heat, melt the chocolate and vegetable shortening, stirring until smooth. Cool slightly.

7 Spoon chocolate over each cluster, being sure to cover completely. Alternatively, using a fork, dip each cluster into chocolate and lift out, tapping on the edge of the saucepan to shake off excess.

8 Place on the wire rack over the baking sheet. Allow to set for 2 hours, until hardened.

Louisiana Pralines

This version of pralines resembles pools of nut fudge and is deliciously indulgent.

Makes 30

❦

INGREDIENTS

2 cups pecan halves
*2 well-packed cups light brown
sugar*
scant 1 cup granulated sugar
1¼ cups whipping cream
¾ cup milk
1 teaspoon vanilla extract

❦

1 Coarsely chop half of the pecans and set all the nuts aside. Line 2–3 baking sheets with baking parchment.

2 Stir both sugars, the cream and milk together in a heavy-bottomed saucepan over medium heat. Stir until the mixture reaches 238°F or the soft ball stage.

3 Remove from the heat immediately and beat with an electric beater or balloon whisk until the mixture loses its sheen and becomes creamy in texture and grainy looking. This could take 15 minutes by hand or about 5 minutes with an electric beater.

4 Stir in the vanilla extract and nuts. Drop tablespoons of the mixture onto the prepared baking sheets, allowing it to spread of its own accord. Allow to cool and set at room temperature. Store between layers of waxed paper in an airtight container.

Chocolate-Coated Nut Brittle

*Equal amounts of pecans and almonds set in crisp caramel, then coated
in semisweet chocolate, make a sensational gift.*

Makes 20–24

❦

INGREDIENTS

*1 cup mixed pecans and whole
almonds
¹/₂ cup sugar
4 tablespoons water
7 ounces semisweet chocolate,
chopped*

❦

Cook's Tip These look best in rough
chunks, so don't worry if the pieces
break unevenly, or if there are gaps in
the chocolate coating.

1 Lightly grease a baking sheet. Mix
the nuts, sugar and water in a
heavy-bottomed saucepan. Place the
pan over low heat, stirring without
boiling until the sugar has dissolved.

2 Bring to a boil, then lower the
heat to medium and cook until
the mixture turns a rich golden
brown and registers 300°F on a
sugar thermometer.

3 To test without a thermometer,
drop a small amount of the
mixture into a cup of ice water. The
mixture should become brittle enough
to snap with your fingers.

4 Quickly remove the pan from the
heat and tip the mixture onto the
prepared baking sheet, spreading it
evenly. Leave until completely cold
and hard.

5 Break the nut brittle into bite-sized
pieces. Melt the chocolate in a
heatproof bowl over a saucepan of
hot water and dip the pieces to
half-coat them. Leave on a sheet of
baking parchment to set.

Chocolate Fudge Triangles

This fudge can be stored in an airtight container in the refrigerator for up to 2 weeks.

Makes 48

INGREDIENTS

*1 pound 5 ounces good-quality
white chocolate, chopped
14 fluid-ounce can sweetened
condensed milk
1 tablespoon vanilla extract
1¹/₂ teaspoons lemon juice
pinch of salt
scant 2 cups hazelnuts or pecans,
chopped (optional)
6 ounces semisweet chocolate,
chopped
3 tablespoons unsalted butter,
chopped
2 ounces semisweet chocolate,
melted, to decorate*

1 Line an 8-inch square baking pan with foil. In a saucepan over low heat, melt the chocolate and condensed milk, stirring frequently. Remove from the heat and stir in the vanilla extract, lemon juice, salt, and nuts, if using. Spread half of the mixture in the pan. Chill for 15 minutes.

2 In a saucepan over low heat, melt the semisweet chocolate and butter, stirring until smooth. Remove from the heat, cool slightly, then pour over the chilled white layer and chill for 15 minutes.

3 Gently reheat the remaining white chocolate mixture and pour over the set semisweet chocolate layer. Smooth the top, then chill for 2–4 hours, until set.

4 Using the foil to lift it, remove the fudge from the pan and turn onto a cutting board. Remove the foil and, using a sharp knife, cut into 24 squares. Cut each square into two triangles. To decorate, drizzle with melted chocolate.

Honey and Nut Clusters

These are popular in Italy. To serve, cut in squares or fingers and keep in the
refrigerator. They are delightfully sticky!

Makes 48

ℐ

INGREDIENTS

²/₃ *cup blanched almonds*
1 cup shelled hazelnuts
whites of 2 eggs
¹/₃ *cup honey*
¹/₂ *cup sugar*

ℐ

1 Preheat the oven to the lowest temperature. Line an 8-inch square pan with baking parchment.

2 Spread the almonds and hazelnuts on separate baking sheets and toast in the oven for about 30 minutes. Turn onto a cloth and rub off the skins. Coarsely chop both types of nut.

3 Beat the egg whites until they are stiff, and stir in the chopped nuts.

4 Put the honey and sugar into a small, heavy-bottomed saucepan and bring to a boil. Stir in the nut mixture and cook over medium heat for 10 minutes.

5 Turn the mixture into the prepared pan and level the top. Cover with another piece of baking parchment, put weights (such as food cans) on top and chill for at least 2 days.

6 To present as a tree decoration, wrap slices in baking parchment and then in gift wrap or cotton fabric, or in foil.

Peppermint and Coconut Chocolate Sticks

Dried coconut gives these chocolate mint sticks a unique flavor and texture.

Makes 80

❧

INGREDIENTS

¹/₂ cup sugar
²/₃ cup water
¹/₂ teaspoon peppermint extract
*7 ounces semisweet dark
chocolate, chopped*
*4 tablespoons toasted dried
coconut*

❧

1 Lightly oil a large baking sheet. Place the sugar and water in a small, heavy-bottomed saucepan and heat gently, stirring occasionally, until the sugar has dissolved completely.

2 Bring to a boil and boil rapidly without stirring until the syrup registers 280°F on a sugar thermometer. Remove the pan from the heat and add the peppermint extract, then pour onto the prepared baking sheet and leave until set and completely cold.

3 Break up the peppermint mixture into a bowl and use the end of a rolling pin to crush it into pieces.

4 Melt the chocolate in a heatproof bowl over a saucepan of hot water. Remove from the heat and stir in the mint pieces and dried coconut.

5 Place a 12 x 10-inch sheet of baking parchment on a flat surface. Spread the mixture over the parchment, leaving a narrow border all around. Allow to set. When firm, use a knife to cut into thin sticks.

Chocolate Peppermint Crisps

If you do not have a sugar thermometer, test cooked sugar for "hard ball stage"
by spooning a few drops into a bowl of cold water; it should form
a hard ball when rolled between your fingers.

Makes 30

❧

INGREDIENTS

¼ *cup sugar*
¼ *cup water*
1 teaspoon peppermint extract
8 ounces semisweet chocolate,
chopped

❧

1 Lightly brush a large baking sheet with unflavored oil. In a saucepan over a medium heat, heat the sugar and water, swirling the pan gently until the sugar dissolves. Boil rapidly to 280°F on a sugar thermometer. Remove the pan from the heat and add the peppermint extract; swirl to mix. Pour onto the prepared baking sheet and allow to set and cool completely.

2 When cold, break into pieces. Place in a food processor fitted with a metal blade and process until fine crumbs form; do not over-process.

3 Line two baking sheets with baking parchment. Place the chocolate in a small heatproof bowl over a small saucepan of hot water. Place over very low heat until the chocolate has melted, stirring frequently until smooth. Remove from the heat and stir in the peppermint mixture.

4 Using a teaspoon, drop small mounds onto the prepared sheets. Using the back of the spoon, spread to 1½-inch rounds. Cool, then refrigerate for about 1 hour, until set. Peel off the paper and store in airtight containers with baking parchment between the layers.

Striped Cookies

These biscuits may be made in different flavors and colors and look wonderful tied in bundles or packed into boxes. Eat them with ice cream or light desserts.

Makes 25

❧

INGREDIENTS

*1 ounce white chocolate, melted
red and green food coloring
2 egg whites
$\frac{1}{3}$ cup sugar
$\frac{1}{2}$ cup all-purpose flour
4 tablespoons unsalted butter, melted*

❧

1 Preheat the oven to 375°F. Line two baking sheets with baking parchment. Divide the melted chocolate in half and add a little food coloring to each half to color the chocolate red and green. Using two waxed paper icing bags, fill with each color chocolate and fold down the tops. Snip off the points.

2 Place the egg whites in a bowl and beat until stiff. Add the sugar gradually, beating well after each addition, to make a thick meringue. Add the flour and melted butter and beat until smooth.

3 Drop four separate teaspoonfuls of the mixture onto the prepared baking sheets and spread into thin rounds. Pipe lines or zigzags of green and red chocolate over each round.

4 Bake one sheet at a time for 3–4 minutes, until pale golden in color. Loosen the rounds with a metal spatula and return to the oven for a few seconds to soften. Have two or three lightly oiled wooden spoon handles at hand.

5 Taking one round cookie out of the oven at a time, roll it around a spoon handle and leave for a few seconds to set. Repeat to shape the remaining cookies. Put the second sheet of cookies in to bake.

6 When the cookies are set, slip them off the spoon handles onto a wire rack. Repeat with the remaining mixture and the red and green chocolate until all the mixture has been used, baking only one sheet of cookies at a time. If the cookies are too hard to shape, simply return them to the oven for a few seconds to soften.

7 When the cookies are cold, tie them together with colored ribbon and pack into boxes, tins or glass jars.

Almond Fingers

A very simple Middle Eastern sweet that is especially popular in Arab countries.

Makes 40–50

INGREDIENTS

1¼ cups ground almonds
½ cup ground pistachios
¼ cup granulated sugar
1 tablespoon rose water
½ teaspoon ground cinnamon
12 sheets of filo pastry, defrosted
½ cup butter, melted
confectioners' sugar for dusting

1 Preheat the oven to 325°F. Butter a baking sheet. Mix together the almonds, pistachios, sugar, rose water and cinnamon.

2 Cut each sheet of filo pastry into four rectangles. Work with one at a time, and cover the remaining rectangles with a damp dish towel.

3 Brush one rectangle with melted butter, and place a teaspoon of the nut filling in the center.

4 Fold the sides and roll into a finger shape. Continue until all the filling has been used.

5 Place the "fingers" on the baking sheet and bake for 30 minutes. Transfer to a wire rack to cool, then dust with confectioners' sugar.

Basbousa

These delicious Middle Eastern coconut sweets can be served either hot as a dessert or cold with tea.

Makes 12

INGREDIENTS

½ cup unsalted butter
¼ cup sugar
½ cup all-purpose flour
1¼ cups semolina
1½ cups grated coconut
¾ cup milk
1 teaspoon baking powder
1 teaspoon vanilla extract
almonds, to decorate
For the syrup
½ cup sugar
⅔ cup water
1 tablespoon lemon juice

1 To make the syrup, place sugar, water and lemon juice in a saucepan, bring to a boil, simmer for 6–8 minutes. Allow to cool, then chill.

2 Preheat the oven to 350°F. Melt the butter in a saucepan. Add the remaining ingredients and mix thoroughly.

3 Pour the cake mixture into a shallow baking pan, flatten the top and bake for 30–35 minutes.

4 Remove the Basbousa from the oven and cut into diamond-shaped pieces. Pour the cold syrup evenly over the top and decorate with an almond placed in each center.

Semolina and Nut Halva

Semolina is a popular ingredient in many desserts and pastries in the Eastern Mediterranean. Here it provides a sponge cake for soaking up a deliciously fragrant spicy syrup.

Makes 20–24

❧

INGREDIENTS

¹/₂ cup unsalted butter
¹/₂ cup sugar
finely grated rind of 1 orange
2 tablespoons orange juice
3 eggs
1 cup semolina
2 teaspoons baking powder
1 cup ground hazelnuts
¹/₂ cup unblanched hazelnuts,
 toasted and chopped
¹/₂ cup blanched almonds, toasted
 and chopped
shredded rind of 1 orange
For the syrup
1¹/₂ cups sugar
2¹/₄ cups water
2 cinnamon sticks, halved
juice of 1 lemon
4 tablespoons orange flower water

❧

1 Preheat the oven to 425°F. Grease and line the bottom of a deep 9-inch square heavy-based cake pan.

2 Lightly cream the butter in a bowl. Add the sugar, orange rind and juice, the eggs, semolina, baking powder and hazelnuts and beat the ingredients together until smooth.

3 Turn into the prepared pan and level the surface. Bake for 20–25 minutes, until just firm and golden. Leave to cool in the pan.

4 To make the syrup, put the sugar in a heavy-bottomed saucepan with the water and cinnamon sticks. Heat until the sugar has dissolved.

5 Bring to a boil and boil hard for 5 minutes. Measure half the syrup in a pitcher and add the lemon juice and orange flower water to it. Pour over the halva. Reserve the remainder of the syrup in the pan.

6 Leave the halva in the pan until the syrup is absorbed, then turn it out onto a plate and cut diagonally into diamond-shaped portions. Sprinkle with the nuts.

7 Boil the remaining syrup until slightly thickened, then pour it over the halva. Sprinkle the shredded orange rind over the cake and serve with lightly whipped cream.

Jeweled Elephants

These stunningly robed elephants make a lovely gift for all ages, or an edible decoration for a special occasion. If you make holes in them before baking, you could use them as original Christmas tree decorations.

Makes 10

❧

INGREDIENTS

*1 quantity Lebkuchen mixture
1 quantity Icing Glaze
red food coloring
8 ounces ready-to-roll sugar paste
small candy-covered
chocolates or chews
gold dragees*

❧

3 Knead some red food coloring into half of the sugar paste. Roll a little red sugar paste under your fingers into ropes. Secure them around the feet and tips of the trunk, using icing from the bag. Shape more red sugar paste into flat oval shapes, about ³/₄ inch long, and stick them to the elephants' heads. Shape smaller ovals and secure them at the top of the trunks.

5 Pipe ¹/₂-inch tassels around the edges. Pipe dots of white icing at the tops of the trunks, around the necks and at the tops of the tails and also use it to draw small eyes. Halve the small chocolates and press the halves into the sugar paste, above the tassels. Decorate the headdress, candies and white sugar paste with gold dragees, securing them with dots of icing. Set aside for several hours, to harden.

1 Preheat the oven to 350°F. Grease two large baking sheets. Make a paper template for the elephant. Roll out the Lebkuchen mixture. Use the template and a sharp knife to cut out elephant shapes. Space them slightly apart on the baking sheet and bake for 3 minutes and then transfer to a wire rack to cool.

2 Put a little Icing Glaze in a paper icing bag fitted with a fine nozzle. Alternatively, cut off the tip of the bag to make a nozzle.

4 Roll out the white sugar paste. Cut out circles, using a 2¹/₂-inch cookie cutter. Secure to the elephants' backs with royal icing so that the edge of the sugar paste is about 1 inch above the top of the legs. Trim off the excess paste around the top of the white sugar paste shapes.

Index

Index

almonds: almond fingers, 248
  almond-topped squares, 170
  amaretti, 86
  apricot and almond fingers, 172
  chocolate almond torronne, 116
  chocolate amaretti, 111
  chocolate-coated nut brittle, 241
  chocolate fruit and nut cookies, 114
  chocolate raspberry macaroon bars, 178
  cinnamon balls, 75
  citrus spice bars, 180
  honey and nut clusters, 243
  macaroons, 88
  Mexican almond cookies, 41
  nut lace cookies, 98
  raspberry sandwich cookies, 103
  slivered almond cookies, 97
  tuiles d'amandes, 96
  vanilla crescents, 70
amaretti, 86
  chocolate amaretti, 111
aniseed cookies, Mexican, 71
apples: apple and cinnamon muffins, 209
  applesauce cookies, 38
  date and apple muffins, 201
  sticky date and apple squares, 174
apricots: apricot and almond fingers, 172
  apricot bars, 173
  apricot meringue bars, 79
  apricot yogurt cookies, 37
  oat and apricot clusters, 219

bacon: bacon cornmeal muffins, 134
  bacon twists, 124
baklava, 74
bananas: banana and nut buns, 196
  banana gingerbread, 158
  banana muffins, 188
  chocolate chip banana pancakes, 211
basbousa, 248
biscotti, 84
biscuits: cheese, 140
  chive and potato, 146
  feta cheese and chive, 143
  ham and sun-dried tomato, 142

sunflower golden raisin, 213
black-and-white ginger florentines, 94
blackberry muffins, 202
blue cheese and chive crisps, 132
blueberries: blueberry muffins, 200
  blueberry streusel slices, 174
  chocolate blueberry muffins, 203
  fruit and cinnamon buns, 196
brandy snaps, 92
Brittany butter cookies, 49
brownies, 150-1
  chocolate, 156
  marbled, 153
  nut and chocolate chip, 157
  raisin, 160
  white chocolate, 152
buns: banana and nut, 196
  fruit and cinnamon, 196
buttermilk: buttermilk cookies, 46
  oatmeal buttermilk muffins, 186
butterscotch bars, chocolate, 162
butterscotch meringue bars, 182

carrot muffins, 198
Cheddar pennies, 130
cheese: blue cheese and chive crisps, 132
  Cheddar pennies, 130
  cheese muffins, 133
  cheese popovers, 136
  cheese biscuits, 140
  cheese straws, 120
  cocktail shapes, 148
  festive nibbles, 120
  feta cheese and chive biscuits, 143
  sablés with goat cheese and strawberries,
    106
  savory cheese whirls, 122
  savory Parmesan puffs, 135
  spiced cocktail biscuits, 149
  tiny cheese puffs, 138
  Wisconsin Cheddar and chive biscuits, 126
cheese, soft: coffee sponge drops, 107
  cream cheese spirals, 123
  lemon cheese bars, 180
cherries: dried cherry muffins, 198
chive and potato biscuits, 146
chocolate: black-and-white ginger
    florentines, 94
  chewy chocolate cookies, 44
  chocolate almond torrone, 116
  chocolate amaretti, 111
  chocolate and coconut slices, 181
  chocolate and nut refrigerator cookies, 57
  chocolate blueberry muffins, 203

chocolate brownies, 156
chocolate butterscotch bars, 162
chocolate chip banana pancakes, 211
chocolate chip hazelnut cookies, 39
chocolate chip muffins, 194
chocolate chip oat cookies, 40
chocolate cinnamon tuiles, 64
chocolate-coated nut brittle, 241
chocolate crackle-tops, 224
chocolate-dipped hazelnut crescents, 93
chocolate dominoes, 225
chocolate fudge triangles, 242
chocolate hazelnut galettes, 117
chocolate kisses, 58
chocolate macaroons, 90
chocolate, maple and walnut swirls, 60
chocolate marzipan cookies, 55
chocolate nut clusters, 238
chocolate pecan squares, 160
chocolate peppermint crisps, 245
chocolate pretzels, 59
chocolate raspberry macaroon bars, 178
chocolate-tipped cookies, 232
chocolate walnut bars, 167
chocolate walnut muffins, 194
chunky chocolate drops, 54
cranberry and chocolate squares, 83
crunchy jumbles, 32
decorated chocolate Lebkuchen, 112
double chocolate chip muffins, 192
double chocolate cookies, 56
fruit and nut clusters, 220
fudge-glazed chocolate slices, 154
marbled brownies, 153
mocha Viennese swirls, 110
nut and chocolate chip brownies, 157
peppermint and coconut chocolate sticks,
    244
tollhouse cookies, 42
white chocolate brownies, 152
white chocolate macadamia slices, 164
Christmas cookies, 81
Christmas trees, jeweled, 82
churros, Spanish, 52
cinnamon: almond cinnamon balls, 75
  apple and cinnamon muffins, 209

Index

chocolate cinnamon tuiles, 64
cinnamon and molasses cookies, 66
cinnamon refrigerator cookies, 67
  fruit and cinnamon buns, 196
  pineapple and cinnamon pancakes, 210
citrus spice bars, 180
cocktail biscuits, spiced, 149
cocktail shapes, 148
coconut: basbousa, 248
  chocolate and coconut slices, 181
  coconut macaroons, 90
  coconut oat cookies, 32
  coconut pyramids, 76
  peppermint and coconut chocolate sticks,
    244
coffee: coffee sponge drops, 107
  mocha Viennese swirls, 110
corn oysters, 126
cornmeal: bacon cornmeal muffins,
    134
  cornmeal biscuits, 128
  golden raisin cornmeal cookies, 86
crackers, curried, 147
cranberry and chocolate squares, 83
cranberry muffins, 190
cream cheese spirals, 123
crisped rice cereal: crunchy jumbles, 32
  marshmallow Krispie cakes, 221
crunchy jumbles, 32
curried crackers, 147

dates: date and apple muffins, 201
  date crunch, 222
  sticky date and apple squares, 174
dill and potato cakes, 145
dominoes, chocolate, 225

Easter cookies, 77
elephants, jeweled, 252

festive nibbles, 120
feta cheese and chive biscuits, 143
fig bars, spiced, 176
five-spice fingers, 233
florentines, black-and-white ginger, 94

fruit and cinnamon buns, 196
fruit and nut clusters, 220
fruit and nut Lebkuchen, 114
fudge triangles, chocolate, 242
fudge-glazed chocolate slices, 154

galettes, chocolate hazelnut, 117
ginger: banana gingerbread, 158
  black-and-white ginger florentines, 94
  double gingerbread cookies, 62
  ginger cookies, 226
  gingerbread jungle, 228
  gingerbread mixture, 62, 80
  gingerbread teddy bears, 234
  glazed ginger cookies, 80
  old-fashioned ginger cookies, 61
gingerbread: banana gingerbread, 158
  gingerbread squares, 159
goat cheese, sablés with strawberries and,
    106
golden pillows, 52
golden raisin cornmeal cookies, 86
granola cookies, 30
Greek festival shortbreads, 79

halva, semolina and nut, 250
ham and sun-dried tomato biscuits, 142
hazelnuts: chocolate chip hazelnut cookies,
    39
  chocolate-dipped hazelnut crescents, 93
  chocolate hazelnut galettes, 117
  hazelnut squares, 169
  honey and nut clusters, 243
  semolina and nut halva, 250
herbs: herb popovers, 136
  whole wheat herb triangles, 144
hermits, 182
honey and nut clusters, 243

Icing glaze, 23
Italian pastry twists, 78

jeweled Christmas trees, 82
jeweled elephants, 252

lace cookies: nut, 98
  oatmeal, 98
ladyfingers, 108
lavender: lavender heart cookies, 69
  lavender scones, 212
Lebkuchen, decorated chocolate, 112
Lebkuchen, fruit and nut, 114
lemon: creamy lemon bars, 176
  lemon cheese bars, 180
  lemon squares, 171
  lemony peanut pairs, 226

Louisiana pralines, 240

macadamia nuts: white chocolate brownies,
    152
  white chocolate macadamia slices, 164
macaroons, 88
  chocolate, 90
  chocolate raspberry bars, 178
  coconut, 90
madeleines, 88
malted oat crisps, 34
maple syrup: chocolate, maple and walnut
    swirls, 60
  maple pecan muffins, 189
marbled brownies, 153
marshmallow krispie cakes, 221
marzipan cookies, chocolate, 55
melting moments, 36
meringue bars: apricot, 79
  butterscotch, 182
Mexican almond cookies, 41
Mexican aniseed cookies, 71
mocha Viennese swirls, 110
molasses cookies, cinnamon and, 66
Moravian tarts, 79
muesli: chewy fruit muesli slice, 218
  granola cookies, 30
muffins, 185
  apple and cinnamon, 209
  bacon cornmeal, 134
  banana, 188
  blackberry, 202
  blueberry, 200
  carrot, 198
  cheese, 133
  chocolate blueberry, 203
  chocolate chip, 194
  chocolate walnut, 194
  cranberry, 190
  date and apple, 201
  double chocolate chip, 192
  dried cherry, 198
  maple pecan, 189
  nutty muffins with walnut liqueur, 208
  oatmeal buttermilk, 186
  prune, 204
  pumpkin, 186
  raisin bran, 206

raspberry, 190
raspberry crumble, 207
yogurt honey, 204
mustard and thyme biscuits, 129

necklaces, sweet, 230
nuts: chocolate-coated nut brittle, 241
chocolate nut clusters, 238
nut and chocolate chip brownies, 157
nut lace cookies, 98
nutty muffins with walnut liqueur, 208
spiced-nut palmiers, 65

oats: banana gingerbread, 158
chocolate chip oat cookies, 40
coconut oat cookies, 32
crunchy oatmeal cookies, 30
gingerbread squares, 159
malted oat crisps, 34
oat and apricot clusters, 219
oatcakes, 140
oatmeal buttermilk muffins, 186
oatmeal lace cookies, 98
oatmeal wedges, 35
oranges: citrus spice bars, 180
orange raisin scones, 214
orange shortbread fingers, 102

palmiers, spiced-nut, 65
pancakes: chocolate chip banana, 211
pineapple and cinnamon, 210
pastries: almond fingers, 248
baklava, 74
Italian pastry twists, 78
savory cheese whirls, 122
spiced-nut palmiers, 65
tiny cheese puffs, 138
peanut butter: lemony peanut pairs, 226
peanut butter cookies, 42
peanuts: peanut cookies, 223
salted peanut cookies, 130
pecans: banana and nut buns, 196
chocolate brownies, 156
chocolate-coated nut brittle, 241
chocolate pecan squares, 160
fudge-glazed chocolate slices, 154
Louisiana pralines, 240
maple pecan muffins, 189
pecan puffs, 105

pecan squares, 168
pecan tassies, 104
pepper cookies, spicy, 68
peppermint: chocolate peppermint crisps,
245
peppermint and coconut chocolate sticks,
244
pineapple and cinnamon pancakes, 210
popovers: cheese, 136
herb, 136
potatoes: chive and potato biscuits, 146
dill and potato cakes, 145
pralines, Louisiana, 240
pretzels, chocolate, 59
prune muffins, 204
pumpkin muffins, 186

raisins: orange raisin scones, 214
golden raisin cornmeal cookies, 86
raisin bran muffins, 206
raisin brownies, 160
sunflower golden raisin biscuits, 213
raspberries: raspberry crumble muffins, 207
raspberry muffins, 190
raspberry jam: chocolate raspberry
macaroon bars, 178
raspberry sandwich cookies, 103
refrigerator cookies, chocolate and nut, 57
refrigerator cookies, cinnamon, 67
rose water thins, 50

sablés with goat cheese and strawberries, 106
salted peanut cookies, 130
scones, 185
lavender, 212
orange raisin, 214
teatime, 212
wholewheat, 214
Scottish shortbread, 51
semolina and nut halva, 250
shortbread, 35
orange shortbread fingers, 102
Scottish shortbread, 51
shortcake cookies, 46
shortcakes, strawberry, 100
snickerdoodles, 44
sour cream streusel bars, 163
Spanish churros, 52
strawberries: sablés with goat cheese and,
106
strawberry shortcakes, 100
streusel bars, sour cream, 163
streusel slices, blueberry, 174
striped cookies, 246
sugar cookies, traditional, 48
sunflower golden raisin biscuits, 213

sweet necklaces, 230

tarts: Moravian tarts, 79
pecan tassies, 104
teatime scones, 212
thyme and mustard biscuits, 129
toffee bars, 166
toffee cookies, 50
tollhouse cookies, 42
tomatoes: ham and sun-dried tomato
biscuits, 142
torronne, chocolate almond, 116
tuiles: chocolate cinnamon tuiles, 64
tuiles d'amandes, 96

vanilla crescents, 70
Viennese swirls, mocha, 110

walnut liqueur, nutty muffins with, 208
walnuts: chewy chocolate cookies, 44
chocolate and nut refrigerator cookies, 57
chocolate, maple and walnut swirls, 60
chocolate walnut bars, 167
chocolate walnut muffins, 194
cream cheese spirals, 123
marbled brownies, 153
nut and chocolate chip brownies, 157
sour cream streusel bars, 163
toffee bars, 166
walnut cookies, 108
whole wheat herb triangles, 144
whole wheat scones, 214
Wisconsin Cheddar and chive biscuits, 126

yogurt: apricot yogurt cookies, 37
yogurt honey muffins, 204

NOTES

NOTES

NOTES

NOTES

NOTES

NOTES

NOTES

NOTES